T0113146

SECULAR
SACRED
SPIRIT

SECULAR

SACRED

SPIRIT

—

BLAKE
K. HEALY

CHARISMA
HOUSE

Most Charisma Media products are available at special quantity discounts for bulk purchase for sales promotions, premiums, fund-raising, and educational needs. For details, call us at (407) 333-0600 or visit our website at www.charismamedia.com.

SECULAR/SACRED/SPIRIT by Blake K. Healy
Published by Charisma House, an imprint of Charisma Media
600 Rinehart Road, Lake Mary, Florida 32746

This book or parts thereof may not be reproduced in any form, stored in a retrieval system, or transmitted in any form by any means—electronic, mechanical, photocopy, recording, or otherwise—without prior written permission of the publisher, except as provided by United States of America copyright law.

Copyright © 2023 by Blake K. Healy
All rights reserved

Visit the author's website at blakekhealy.com.

Cataloging-in-Publication Data is on file with the Library of Congress.
International Standard Book Number: 978-1-63641-115-6
E-book ISBN: 978-1-63641-116-3

While the author has made every effort to provide accurate internet addresses at the time of publication, neither the publisher nor the author assumes any responsibility for errors or for changes that occur after publication. Further, the publisher does not have any control over and does not assume any responsibility for author or third-party websites or their content.

23 24 25 26 27 — 987654321
Printed in the United States of America

For Beni Johnson—a friend who saw the best in me before I could see it for myself

sec·u·lar | \ˈse-kyə-lər \

a: of or relating to the worldly or temporal
b: not overtly or specifically religious
c: not ecclesiastical or clerical

sa·cred | \ ˈsā-krəd \

1a: dedicated or set apart for the service or worship of a deity
b: devoted exclusively to one service or use (as of a person or purpose)
2a: worthy of religious veneration: HOLY
b: entitled to reverence and respect
3: of or relating to religion: not secular or profane

spir·it | \ ˈspir-ət \

1: an animating or vital principle held to give life to physical organisms
2: a supernatural being or essence: such as
a: *capitalized* : HOLY SPIRIT
3: the immaterial intelligent or sentient part of a person[1]

CONTENTS

INTRODUCTION

THE FIRST THING I saw when I woke up this
morning was an angel. It stood no more than
a step away from where I was sleeping, gathering small things from the ground and stuffing
them into a pillowcase-sized bag. The inquisitive
part of my mind wanted to know what it was picking
up, why it was collecting it, and how anything that
would be significant to an angel ended up on my
bedroom floor amongst the discarded laundry next
to my bed. But a lifetime of seeing this kind of thing
has taught me that patience is the first key to understanding the things you see in the spirit.

I kicked myself out of bed, gathered up an assortment of suitable clothing, and jumped in the shower.

The angel continued following me around, picking up things here and there, as I brushed my teeth, shaved, and engaged in all the other thrilling components of my morning routine.

I took a moment to look more closely at the things the angel was putting into the bag. A gold-plated screwdriver, a pristine red and yellow apple, a brightly glowing pellet that looked like a multi-vitamin from a science fiction movie; they were all very different, and each carried a sense of metaphorical significance, but trying to comprehend that significance felt like pressing to remember a word just outside the edge of memory, within reach yet frustratingly unobtainable.

I flicked on some worship music with my phone. Instantly another dozen or so of the glowing pellets appeared in the air around me, each in a different phosphorescent shade of blue, green, or yellow. They floated down, slower than snow, landing on the sink, counter, floor, and me, absorbing into my skin like water into a sponge. Immediately, the familiar peace-filled warmth of the presence of God spread across my chest, making it easy to take my time as I finished preparing for the day.

Several minutes later, realizing I was not entirely sure how long I had been lost in the slow comfort of enjoying God's presence, my hand snapped down to my phone, revealing that my languid pace had given me less than three minutes to make it out the door. All sense of warmth and comfort burst with this sudden spike of cold reality. I sprayed a dollop of whatever hair product was within reach, dragged two clawed sets of fingers through my hair until it looked like I had at least tried, and threw on the first presentable set of clothing I could find.

The angel followed me around during this whole process, making sure to grab up all the little pellets of presence (if that is what they were) that had fallen on the counter or ground. It grabbed a few more things that I didn't take time to notice as I grabbed my work bag and pulled on my shoes. I decided to wait to tie my shoes until I got to the car, my frenzied brain convinced that this would somehow save some time.

A quick look at my phone revealed that I still had a minute and a half to make it out the door. I was reeling with satisfaction at my ability to hustle in a pinch, when I heard a soft voice from down the hall.

"Hey, Dad, what's for breakfast?"

I suppressed the urge to reach for the favorite tool of all dads in a hurry, *go ask your mom*, and instead said, "Uh...toast," figuring that was fast enough.

I had forgotten that it was my turn to get up and make breakfast, and though I certainly could have asked my wife to wake up and fill in the gap

I had left, missing out on an extra fifteen minutes of sleep is not a small ask when you are in a family with five kids. Plus, only one of the kids was up; make some toast, put some jam and butter on the table, the rest of the kids wake up and make their own breakfast, April wakes up with a warm sense of gratitude for her ever-so-thoughtful husband—a flawless plan.

Unfortunately, three more kids were awake before the first batch of toast popped, each with requests for various flavors of jam, levels of toastiness, and different kinds of bread. Just as I finished the last of these surprisingly specific orders, kid number five walked down the stairs asking if it is OK to mix Nutella, strawberry jam, and mayonnaise.

"Nope," I said in a flat tone, "it is against the law." I meant it as a joke, of course, but my son's half smile and drifting eye contact made it clear that more than a little of my souring mood had leaked into my tone.

I turned and saw the angel holding the golden screwdriver it had picked up in my room earlier. As soon as I recognized it, the angel thrust forward like it was holding a dagger and slammed the screwdriver into the top of my hand. I didn't feel a thing, and though it looked like the screwdriver should have pinned my hand to the countertop, I could move my hand without issue.

I suddenly remembered that I had been listening to a parenting podcast while going to bed the previous night. The people on it had been talking about how important it is to have healthy boundaries with our kids, even with things that are intended to be kind and loving. Otherwise, we are unable to protect our ability to remain kind and loving in our attitude toward them. I am sure more than a few parents have already been trying to shout this message to me through the pages of this book.

I don't have time, in this introductory story, to dive into how my early childhood experience taught me, among many other things, that it is unloving to say no to doing something kind for someone you care about; or how that simple, seemingly innocuous learning has created flaws in my parenting, friendships, and other relationships.

What I can say is that in this moment of learning—with my son's hurt eyes looking up at me, the piece of revelation from the podcast echoing in my mind, my neck tensed with the stress of the ticking clock, and a golden screwdriver stuck through my hand—I understood how I could grow.

I knelt to meet my son at eye level and apologized for the way I spoke to him, explained that I was stressed because I was late for work, and let him know that I would set out everything for breakfast and then leave so that I could avoid being any later. The golden screwdriver liquefied, absorbing into my hand as easily as the pellets of light from before. A lesson learned, a new relational tool incorporated into my mindset, a heavenly impartation of wisdom; I wasn't sure if the screwdriver represented one, all, or any of these things, only that it represented something good integrating itself into my life.

I sent a quick text to the people in the meeting I was late for, feeling my emotions ping-pong between disappointment at myself for the way I spoke to my son and the disvalue I was communicating to my coworkers. As if in response to this, the angel pulled out the apple it had taken from next to my bed and pressed it into my chest. Like the lights and the screwdriver, it sank into my chest with ease. A sense of comfort mixed in with the introspective frustration, making it easier to learn from the mistakes rather than beat myself up for them.

Was the apple an impartation of comfort? A gift from heaven? Something I couldn't have gotten without the angel's help? I didn't know—not yet, anyway.

I finished setting everything up for the kids, kissed each of them goodbye, and made my way out the door.

I pulled into the parking lot at work a little over fifteen minutes late, not too shabby all things considered. The meeting I had been late for ended up being delayed half an hour, so the toast and jam fiasco hadn't been nearly as disastrous as expected. I walked upstairs to my office, sat down at my desk, and took the few extra minutes to remind myself of all the meetings and tasks that had been assigned to the day. Doing this triggered a sudden and desperate urge for a strong cup of coffee. I leapt from my chair and nearly smashed my office door into the face of a middle-aged man in blue coveralls.

I apologized for my careless abandon in the pursuit of coffee, and he introduced himself.

"Just here to check the wiring in some of these new lights," he said as he lifted a hand to the rows of recessed lighting in the ceiling.

I've never been the best at small talk. Don't get me wrong; I love people. I've never met anyone who wasn't worth knowing. I've just never managed to get particularly good at the getting-to-know-you part.

I put on my friendliest smile and said something witty and insightful like, "Yep, lights sure are important."

He matched my smile and paused for a moment, probably searching for a polite way to respond to my empty remark when another, younger man walked in.

"Ah, this here's my boy," he said, injecting a surprising amount of fatherly pride into the last word.

His son nodded, giving only a moment of polite eye contact before focusing all attention on the bag of tools he set on the counter.

Though the man's son looked no older than thirty, something about his guarded posture and grim expression made him look at least as old as his father—older in some ways.

Without much thought, I took a split second to look at the son in the spirit. He was covered in dozens of thick scars. His knuckles were swollen and scarred over. He looked skinnier than in real life too, malnourished. The old scars were intersected with fresh open cuts and dark blue bruises across his face and arms, like he had just lost a knife fight in a broom closet.

A wave of compassion flooded into my heart, as it always does when I see the spiritual manifestations of the pain people have endured. Everything in me wanted to give comfort and acceptance to this man, but honestly, I had no idea how to do that with someone I had only just met.

Taking my prolonged silence as another example of the social awkwardness I had displayed earlier, the father filled the quiet. "Yeah, we, uh, just got the opportunity to work together. I love it."

Again, the father's tone emanated a deep and profound love for his son, but this time an edge of sadness came through just as clearly. Though I could not have guessed at the details, the shape of this father-son story quickly outlined itself in my mind. It looked something like the story of the prodigal son, only with all the nuances and imperfections that storytellers usually polish away. It was the prodigal son with a less-than-perfect father and consequences for the son's actions that last beyond his return home.

Sensing this only deepened the feeling of compassion and added to my frustration at not knowing how to express the compassion I felt to the people in front of me. I said something awkward about how good it is to work with family, insisted that I didn't want to get in the way of their work, and then grabbed my cup of coffee and retreated into my office.

I kept glancing up through the window as the father and son did their work, feeling guilty about not doing something in response to the son's pain. An angel stood next to the father as he held the ladder steady for his son, who was pulling wiring through an opening. A multicolored fire was burning between the father and the son as they worked. The fire flowed between them with the characteristics of arcing electricity but the organic consuming flow of active flame. The fire caught on each of the son's wounds and scars, healing rather than consuming, turning wound to scar and scar to fresh and tender skin. The angel walked around them with a prod in his hand, tending the flames, pressing at places on the father and son.

Seeing the healing that was happening in front of me brought some comfort to my earlier frustration. It is humbling to realize that you don't have the solution to every problem, even the problems that you can see and understand.

I sat for a moment, thinking about the first part of my day, when a question occurred to me, one that comes up often when I take consistent notice of what is happening in the spirit around me: What was the most spiritually significant thing that happened today? Was it the moment of worship I had when I was getting ready for work? Was it the adjustment I made with the way I was treating my children? Was that caused by good information from a podcast? Or was it a spiritual impartation from heaven? Was my parental moment more spiritually significant than this father and son changing out a light? Would the son have been more healed if I prayed for him or gave him a prophetic word? Or was working with his father a higher form of spiritual healing?

It's hard to say, really. I have been seeing in the spirit all my life and still I wonder, What is secular? What is sacred? And what is spirit?

———

Now, any reasonable person is likely to arrive at the end of this story with at least a few questions of their own:

- Why was there a bunch of spiritual debris all over your bedroom?

- Were those pellets of light God's presence or worship or something?

- Why did the angel have to pick that stuff up?

- What would have happened if the angel didn't pick it up?

- What caused that man's wounds?

- Do I have wounds?

- Was his dad healing his wounds?

- Was the angel healing them?

- Are you really asking me to believe that an angel stabbed you in the hand with a golden screwdriver to help improve your parenting?

I have been teaching, speaking, and writing about seeing in the spirit for nearly eighteen years, and in that time, people have asked me a lot of questions. The span and variety of these questions has grown with each passing year, from specific inquiries like the ones listed above, to broader philosophical questions such as the following:

- Why is so much of what you see so metaphorical?

- Do the things that happen in the spirit realm affect us?

- Do we affect them?

- Is this stuff really real?

- Is it just an abstract idea?

- If it is real, why can't most people see it?

Whether the questions are broad and conceptual or specific and concrete, almost all of them can be boiled down to one fundamental question:

- How does the spirit realm work?

It's a simple question, and it has a simple answer. It's the main question we will be exploring as we walk together through the rest of this book, and by the end, I hope that you will not only understand my answer, but that you will also have one of your own. I also hope that by the end of this book, you will understand the spirit realm so well that you will be able to answer all the questions above without me having to explain any further at all.

———

One question that you might need answered before we get too much further is, What do you mean by "spirit realm"?

The full answer is one that is explored across the breadth of this book, so I will not try to approach it from that angle, but I will give you a starting point. When I say *spirit realm*, I am talking about the part of reality where angels and demons abide, where the spiritual part of each of us exists and God's presence is manifest.

Also, I use the term in a largely academic sense. I am not saying that the spirit realm itself is purely abstract, metaphorical, or just an intangible idea; only that creating a distinction between the spirit and physical world is, in my opinion, a purely academic exercise.

God created the world and everything in it. The spirit realm is as much a part of the physical world as gravity, mathematics, and the laws of physics.

Separating these concepts from one another is helpful as we try to understand their relationship to each other, but they are only separate in our minds. So it is with the spirit realm.

In past books I have described a difference between the spirit realm, soul realm, and physical realm. Again, creating a distinction between the spirit, the soul (your mind, will, and emotions), and your body is helpful for building an understanding, but it can draw a picture of separation that is far from accurate. The biologist can create distinctions between your body's nervous and circulatory systems, but we understand that these systems (along with many others) function together so completely that they are just as much a part of one another as they are separate. So it is with the spirit realm and the way you fit into it.

So, is it a different plane of existence? Is it the kingdom of heaven? Is that something that's inside the spirit realm, or is the spirit realm something that is inside of it? Is this where angels and demons battle it out for the fate of mankind? If it's literal, then how literal is it? A lot of the things you talk about sound metaphorical; doesn't that mean it's all just a big metaphor?

All good questions, and again, I believe that by the end of this book you will have answers to each one.

But I must ask—and I know it is a very large thing to ask—for a certain degree of patience.

My goal with this book is to pretend that you and I (whoever, wherever, and whenever you are) are going on a walk together, talking about seeing in the spirit and the spirit realm. To achieve this, I have structured this book in a way that is often meandering and conversational. Some of you may find this frustrating at times (perhaps you already are), but please know that this is intentional and, I feel, necessary. The spirit realm is not complicated, but it is complex. Trying to explain everything detail by detail or give you a systematic approach to understanding the spirit realm would, counterintuitively, make it more difficult to comprehend.

I'm reminded of a visit I paid to my father-in-law's house one summer. He is a magnificent gardener, and getting to eat fresh raspberries, zucchini, and lettuce from his garden is one of the highlights of every visit. I walked with him one day as he was tending the garden to ask him questions about how he grew such delicious food, hoping that my wife and I could start a garden of our own.

He began describing how to tell when tomatoes are ripe, nearly ripe, and overripe just by the shade of their skin. He held up three different handfuls of leaves, explaining how each indicated whether the plant had enough water or sun or good strong roots. He pressed a thumb gently into the surface of a squash saying how it should feel when it's time to harvest.

At first I tried to take mental notes of each detail; the difference between the shades of ripe or unripe tomatoes, the texture of thirsty leaves. After a while I wished I had brought a notebook out with me. Before long I realized that even three notebooks wouldn't have been enough. It suddenly occurred to me that my father-in-law had not learned how to be a great gardener by memorizing details. He became a great gardener by walking through the garden with his father, day in and day out, talking and learning.

Learning about seeing in the spirit and the spirit realm is like learning about gardening. I am not your father (unless one of my kids happens to be reading this), and I am not coming to you under the pretext of being an expert of any kind, but I have been walking through this particular garden for a long time. And I would love to talk to you about it, not just because it is exciting and beautiful, but because when we explore this garden, we learn a lot about the master gardener who planted it in the beginning and tends to it every day.

So let's walk together. We'll step in and out of parts of my story. I'll share about what I know of how the spirit realm works. We'll talk about how to understand the language of heaven. And we'll explore the difference between what is secular, what is sacred, and what you are as a spirit in this vast and wonderful garden.

CHAPTER 1

MY STORY, PART 1

FOR THE FIRST few years, I didn't know that I was seeing in the spirit. I saw angels every day, but they fit so well with everything else exciting and new in my ever-widening view of the world that I didn't know they were anything other than ordinary. They walked alongside people, whispering things in their ears, resting comforting hands on their shoulders, smiling at their jokes, weeping at their sorrows, or waiting patiently for their services to be required.

I could tell they weren't people. Their clothes blew in wind that I couldn't feel. They passed through solid walls and things as if they weren't there. They could walk on the air as easily as solid ground. Their skin looked like it was made of sunshine. And at least half of them had wings. I could tell they weren't people, but there are a lot of things in the world other than people, and when you are young, you see things for the first time almost every day.

I saw demons too. They looked scary, of course, but I was almost never scared of them. I guess that's not totally true; they did scare me, but in the same way that an angry man on the far side of the street was scary, or a big dog on the other side of a fence. These things were scary, but scary at a distance.

I talked about the angels and demons I saw, but this was usually dismissed as the product of an active imagination. As I grew older, gentle social pressures caused me to talk about the things I saw less and less. A three-year-old talking about a lady dressed in gold dancing on the ceiling will earn an indulgent smile and a ruffle on the head, but even by five or six the subtle pain of receiving an odd look from a friend or family member was more than enough to keep me from bringing up most of what I saw. I remember thinking that it must be rude to talk about those kinds of things.

This mutual ignorance continued through most of my early childhood. Once I started getting old enough to get a firmer grasp on the difference between reality and imagination, I started to realize that not everyone saw the same things that I did. Unfortunately, these early seeds of thought didn't have the opportunity to grow into any clearer understanding, because the way I experienced the things I saw changed dramatically just after I turned nine.

One night, just a few minutes after my mother had finished tucking me into bed, a shadow came into my room. It was vaguely the shape of a person but made of a smeared darkness more solid than air and less substantial than smoke. As it walked to the end of my bed, a pair of milky white eyes flashed near the place where its face should be, and a fear more overpowering than any I had ever experienced in my short life overwhelmed me from head to toe. I couldn't move; I couldn't breathe; I could only stay frozen in place, an unwilling contestant in a staring contest with unrelenting terror.

I don't recall being afraid of anything in particular. I wasn't afraid that I was going to die. I wasn't afraid that I was going to be hurt. But still my entire body was locked in an endless and aimless panic, like a shocked hand unable to let go of a live wire.

It's hard to remember how long I was stuck in that petrifying state—five minutes, an hour; either seems just as likely—but after some time, I found that I was able to move my shoulders. With another few minutes of effort I was able to rock my shoulders back and forth enough to build up the momentum needed to flip myself over facedown in my pillow. I was asleep within a few breaths.

I woke up the next morning with a jolt, but the demon or shadow or whatever it was had gone, taking the weight of fear along with it. I saw the same number of angels and demons I normally would as I went about the business of being a nine-year-old all that day. Though the memory of the previous night's encounter gave me pause each time I saw a demon resting on a person's shoulder or a dark, shadowy figure slithering through the sky, seeing them did not strike me with the same paralyzing fear. By the end of the day, I was beginning to hope that the entire ordeal had been an especially vivid nightmare—that is, until my mom walked me to my room and I saw the shadow at the foot of my bed, waiting for me.

Every night after that there was something new in my room, every night something more frightening than the night before, every night the electric fear overwhelmed my senses, and every night it got worse. This lasted for three and a half years.

A more detailed account of this part of my life is contained in my first book, *The Veil*. Feel free to seek it there if you're curious, or if hearing my story helps you make peace with your own. Just know that I do not breeze past these three years of fear, confusion, and pain because I think it's too scary or dangerous. I move through here quickly because the longer I have walked out my life, the smaller this part of my life has become.

We'll discuss a few insights and lessons about this time in the following chapter, but that's about it.

I did, however, want to take this moment to step outside the narrative and address anyone who is currently or has ever gone through something like what I've described. I used to think that I was the only person who was going through this kind of torment and fear. Now that I have been speaking publicly about this for so many years, I know that there are hundreds and hundreds of people just like me and just like you. You are not the least bit alone; you just probably live in a place where it feels safer to hide this part of your life. I cannot tell you whether you're in a safe place to process this. But what I can say is that it will not be this way forever, and you will one day look back on this part of your story and see it as a small part of something grand. I sincerely hope that this book will be a part of making that come true.

Now, back to my story.

I wasn't sure if I was losing my mind or if the devil had suddenly decided to ruin my life. Either way, my situation grew more hopeless by the day. I was too frightened to tell my parents what I was seeing. Anytime I imagined doing so, my mind was quickly filled with images of myself strapped to a bed in a room with soft white walls. So instead, I just told them that I was afraid.

My parents were devout Christians. They prayed

for me each night, gave me scriptures to quote when I felt scared, and played soft worship music in my room, but nothing helped. Every night some new horror was waiting. Every night I struggled through layers of terror to find my way to sleep.

Reprieve from this accelerating cycle of fear came just after I turned twelve. My family and I moved across the country and started going to a new church. Some of the churches we attended had talked about the gifts of the Spirit and hearing God's voice, but any discussion about this topic was either too academic or too mysterious to become practical in my mind. This new church was different.

They taught regularly about the gifts of the Spirit and how all Christians were intended to have access to them, especially the gift of prophecy. God's voice had always, in my understanding, been relegated to the extremes of either hearing a booming voice coming from the sky or a quiet internal whisper nearly indistinguishable from intuition. The former only ever happened to missionaries in dangerous foreign lands who found themselves in life-threatening situations, and the latter was usually the domain of hyper-religious church people who wanted divine confirmation for their own desires and ideas.

The picture of prophecy painted by these new church leaders was vastly different. To them, prophecy had far greater nuance than simply being an audible voice or the gentle press of intuition. Visions could be as dramatic and vivid as a hologram or as simple and subtle as a single image appearing in the forefront of your imagination. God's voice could come to you as clear as a well-tuned radio or as a delicate and inaudible whisper in the depths of your heart. He could speak through an impression, a scripture, or a coincidence, or by simply dropping a piece of knowledge directly into your mind.

Though the skeptical part of me thought this was too broad and potentially flaky, some part of it resonated with my heart profoundly. The idea that God, almighty and all-knowing, wanted to talk to me directly was at the same time too good to be true and too good not to be. Though nothing they taught about described my exact experience, there was a similarity that I could not place but could not deny.

It gave me enough courage to tell my parents the full extent of what I was experiencing. They took me to speak with some of the prophetic ministers at the church, and for the first time I heard about a gift that they called seeing in the spirit. And within a week the nighttime terrors stopped completely.

At the time I wasn't sure exactly what had caused them to stop. I told someone the truth about what was happening to me, learned that God wanted to talk to me, and discovered that the things I saw were not just an attack but the result of a gift that I hadn't learned how to use yet; something in that recipe had closed the door of fear that had been stuck open for three years. I wasn't sure why or how, but at that point I didn't care; I was just glad that it was closed.

———

My memories of the weeks that followed have stirred themselves together over the years, causing me to recall them now as one long montage. Every day I would take time to pay special attention whenever I saw an angel or demon. I'd take note of what they were wearing, what they were doing, and what this implied about their intention and purpose.

Those angels are wearing long, brightly colored robes, and they dance and sing whenever a worship song comes on; they must be worship angels. These angels wear suits of armor and carry weapons; they must be protection or warrior angels. This demon has oversized eyes that constantly dart around in paranoid little patterns; it must be a demon of fear or anxiety.

Much of what I saw made sense. Things looked like what they were—at least that was how it seemed— but not everything I saw was so intuitive. One day, while our pastor was praying for a group of people, I saw an orangish, reddish, bluish smear of light appear in the room that was somewhat solid, par- tially gaseous, and maybe just a bit liquid in places.

It rushed through the group of people, churning around them in the way of a semisolid, nearly gaseous liquid. It moved through them two or three times then promptly flowed out a high window.

This was so abstract and strange that I couldn't even begin to guess what it meant or what I should do about it. Was that the pastor's prayers? Was it the presence of the Holy Spirit? Was it some kind of spiritual debris being blown by spiritual wind? No idea made more sense than the other.

Much of what I saw made intuitive sense, but just as much was abstract and confusing. I shared the things I saw with our pastor whenever it seemed like a good idea. He was always polite about it, but I could tell that he was confused about what I saw just as often as I was.

I didn't find this too disappointing at first. I was still learning so much about how to operate in this gift. When I was younger, there seemed to be no pattern to when I would see in the spirit and when I wouldn't. Seeing in the spirit was as far outside my control as the weather. It came and went as it pleased. But now that I was practicing so often, I was beginning to feel more in control of when I saw and when I didn't.

Before long it was no different than looking through a window. You can look straight through the glass to the trees or buildings or whatever sits just outside, or you can focus on the glass itself, where you will find any number of water spots, particles of dust, or (if you are at my house) small handprints made of dried-up jam. Both layers of things are always there, but you can choose to focus on one or the other. Within a few months, seeing in the spirit was just as simple. It took much longer, however, to learn to interpret the things that I saw.

My first real breakthrough came after a few solid months of consistent practice. I was sitting at the front of our church, next to my parents, feeling slightly bored. Announcements about ladies' luncheons are not the most thrilling subject for most twelve-year-old boys, so I took the opportunity to see what was happening in the spirit.

Three angels wearing flowing turquoise robes were standing to one side of the stage. They had been dancing all over the room during worship, so I assumed they must be waiting for some song that was going to be played later in the service.

A couple of demons stood huddled together in a far corner. They were short, bone thin, and coal gray, and each movement they made was shaky and unstable, almost like they were sick. They had been wandering around before worship started, their spindly hands reaching out as people walked by, grabbing at their legs. I wasn't sure exactly what they were up to, just that they were looking for an opportunity to be up to something, grasping at each person to see if they could get a grip. They had all sprinted to the corner as soon as the first note of worship rang out through the sanctuary.

There were another dozen or so spiritual things at different parts of the room, but none of them stuck out in a way that caught my attention—not until my eyes landed on an angel near the front of the room.

I had seen the angel every week since we started coming to this church. He was always standing at the same spot, just to the side of the front entrance of the sanctuary. He was medium height, wearing immaculately cared-for silver armor, held a spear in his right hand, and had a short salt-and-pepper beard. He looked like he was in his midfifties. (I'm not sure if an angel can actually be in its midfifties, or even be a *he*, for that matter, but it's what he looked like.)

I stared at him for a long moment. He stood sentinel, unmoving, staring into the distance, everything about his posture and appearance evoking the idea of a guard. On the surface the purpose of this angel seemed obvious. He's a guard, standing at the door, protecting us from...what, exactly?

I turned and looked at the little cluster of shaky demons in the corner. If there was a guard, how did the demons get in? I hadn't seen them arrive. Did they sneak in through a window? Do demons need to sneak in through windows? Did they walk right past the angel? For that matter, what would the angel do to stop the demons? Would he hit them? Would they resist? Would a high-flying kung fu fight ensue, the results of which determine whether God's plans or the devil's plans come to fruition? Beyond that, what was the point of there being a guard? God is our protector, right? What additional protection does an angel provide? No matter how extensive that protection, wouldn't it be redundant in the face of the power of the almighty God?

As I rolled all these questions around in my mind, I suddenly had a vision. I had learned a lot about visions over the past few months. A vision might be open, like the angel I was seeing with my physical eyes, but it might be internal, a sudden divine projection onto the silver screen of your imagination. This was the latter.

A small story passed through my mind, like a memory of a short film I had never seen. I saw two neighboring kingdoms. The king of one of the kingdoms sent an ambassador to the foreign kingdom. With this ambassador he sent a small honor guard, around fifty soldiers. They walked with the ambassador along the road, but when they came to the foreign kingdom, I saw that many hundreds of soldiers were stationed along the walls surrounding their city, and inside there were hundreds more.

If the foreign army decided to attack this ambassador, there is no way that the honor guard would have been able to stop them. Why send the honor guard at all? Maybe they were only intended to protect the ambassador while he was on the road between kingdoms. Despite the intuitive sense this made, I immediately realized that these guards served a much larger purpose.

The guard's presence was not just about the practical protection they provided; it was a statement. The king who had sent the ambassador was saying to all in the foreign kingdom and to anyone the ambassador encountered along the way, "My power goes with this person."

After seeing this play through my mind, I turned and looked at the angel in silver armor again. Nothing about him looked different than before, but I was suddenly seeing every detail in a different light. The immaculate condition of his armor spoke of the intentionality and care he had for the assignment he had been given and the devotion he had for the one who had given it to him. The steadiness of his posture, the appearance of age— all these details painted a rich and nuanced picture of the value that God had for what happened within these walls. It conveyed one layer of value that God's protection and presence would abide in this place. Sending a dedicated servant to preside there as well was not redundant; it deepened the communication of value.

This was the first time I truly felt like I was *understanding* something that I saw. And though I wouldn't have known to describe it this way at the time, it was the first time I realized that I was not just learning how to use a gift; I was learning a new language.

CHAPTER 2

THE LANGUAGE OF HEAVEN, PART 1

L ANGUAGE IS ONE of the most precious gifts we have been given. The ability to understand the thoughts of another person through a simple exchange of sounds or a collection of letters organized in a pattern—wow. Language is part of every day of every person's life. Because of this, it can be easy to skim the surface of understanding language without realizing the incredibly complex feat we are all engaging in.

Let's look at an example. This is going to take a minute, but please trust me—understanding language is one of the most important keys to understanding the spirit realm and the way we experience it.

Someone walks up and says, "You look cool today."

It's a simple phrase. Yeah, there's one piece of slang in there, *cool*, but this word has been around a relatively long time for a slang word, and its definition hasn't changed that much. There are around seven different definitions for the word *cool* in many English dictionaries, but most of you probably heard it similarly given the context provided by the other words. You probably took it to mean very good or hip/fashionable.

So how do the nuances of this single word change based on who is saying it? What subtle differences would you hear if a sixty-five-year-old jazz musician said this to you versus a fifteen-year-old girl with pink hair and a crop top? The same word would mean something similar yet at the same time entirely different. Moreover, who this is being said to makes a big difference as well. If you're a fifty-year-old insurance salesman, you are going to receive this same word from these two people differently than a thirty-five-year-old mother of three.

Even if you just take the fifteen-year-old-girl version of this compliment and imagine how a twelve-year-old girl, another fifteen-year-old girl, or a fifteen-year-old boy would experience it, you can see that who is hearing dramatically changes the underlying experience and meaning.

All this variation exists without even getting into all the other nuances that come from tone, body language, and the further context of where and when this phrase is said.

This example shows us three important things we will need to know going forward:

1. Language is far more than the sum of all the words in a dictionary. It is incredibly intricate and deep.

2. Language is both formed by and constantly affected by our personal culture and history, as well as the culture and history of the world around us, both in big and small ways.

3. Despite all this complexity, we are really good at understanding language.

Even though it took us several paragraphs to break down some of the nuances of language around just one word, if you had been in any of those situations, you would have interpreted all those details and many more nearly instantaneously. Also, even though you may not be a fifteen-year-old boy, a mother of three, or an insurance salesman, you were probably instantly able to imagine how they would experience any of the scenarios I listed. You are designed for language.

Learning to understand the spirit realm is not just like learning a language; it *is* learning a language, the language of heaven. When I say language of heaven, I am not just talking about a way of speaking; I am talking about the language of the kingdom of heaven, communication that is born out of its history and culture, which originate in the heart and mind of God and are perfectly manifested in Jesus Christ.

Learning a language like this may seem like a lofty, even impossible goal. Even suggesting that God has a heart and a mind involves placing limits on His nature that may be entirely misguided. This is the dichotomy of the relationship God has welcomed us into. He has invited us to know the unknowable, to live intimately with He who is supremely holy, to be finite image bearers of an infinite being.

Success in this area requires that we are willing to humble ourselves and let God reveal His language to us. Language is birthed out of culture and history. We are not just learning the right words. We are not memorizing a list of angel associations (armor = warrior angel, dancing = worship angel, yellow = joy, purple = royalty, and so on). We are learning a culture and a history.

To illustrate how language is so intimately tied to culture and history, let me take a moment to tell you about an aboriginal language spoken in Australia called Guugu Yimithirr. This language has no equivalent words for *left* and *right*. Instead, they describe all orientation in relation to the cardinal directions:

north, south, east, and west. So a speaker of this language would not say, "The man standing on your right," but would say, "The man standing to the east of you." If indicating a certain window in a room, someone would say, "The window to the north." If giving instructions to a driver, the person would say, "Turn west here," instead of, "Turn right."

This may seem like a much more complicated way to communicate, but it is not. Language tends to naturally develop toward efficiency (hence all the contractions in this book that may be deeply annoying my grammar-oriented friends). It may not seem efficient to us to describe direction this way, but we must remember language is birthed out of history and culture.

The Guugu Yimithirr language developed in a culture that has had a deep value and need for orienteering. Developing a sense of direction was essential for both survival and success. Knowledge of direction is so deeply instilled from a young age that it would be less efficient for them to think of things in terms of left and right.

There are hundreds of big and small examples of this kind of phenomenon throughout all human language, but I will let you seek those out on your own if you want. For now it is only important that you understand that culture and history shape language.

CODEBOOKS

This idea of the language of heaven is important because there is more than one dialect, if you will, that we can choose when learning to understand the spirit realm. These dialects come with their own set of codebooks, standard interpretations, and common knowledge that all can have a profound effect on how we experience the spirit realm.

I get a wide variety of responses when I share about how I experienced three and a half years of demonic torment, and each response shows a strong sense of the kind of dialect and codebook the person has for the demonic.

Some say, "You must have opened some kind of door. Was there sin in your life? Did you watch too many demonic movies?"

This codebook operates under the pretense that demonic attack can only occur because of personal fault. I committed a very average number of sins between the ages of nine and twelve. I hardly ever watched even mildly scary movies, both because my parents were very careful with what they let me watch and my nighttime experiences made anything designed to cause fear immediately unappealing. Under this spiritual dialect I could easily begin to build a belief that any of those sins or indeed any sin is enough to open my life up to a full-fledged demonic assault. Maybe this is so, but it doesn't seem to leave the gospel with very much power.

Others say, "Were there any witches living in your neighborhood? Or Masons, hippies, Hindus, psychics, new agers, or people playing *Dungeons & Dragons*?"

This codebook comes from a lens that views evil demonic powers creeping around from all directions, needing only the smallest invoking to slither into your life and wreak havoc. While I can't be entirely sure that my neighbors weren't witches (there was one lady who always gave me dirty looks, but I think this had more to do with the fact that I kept riding my bike across her lawn on my way home), this spiritual dialect takes almost all the authority out of my hands and, troublingly, out of God's hands and places it in the hands of the enemy and those who serve him. Seems like the kind of spiritual dialect and codebook the devil would appreciate.

The other common response when people hear my story is, "Well, you just have such a big gifting and calling on your life that the enemy was trying to destroy it."

This codebook, in some ways, comes with the most problems. It comes from a worldview where the devil is permitted to attack you in direct proportion to how God calls and blesses you. This either creates a scenario where you lay low and avoid the gifts and calling of God to avoid pain or a mindset that expects and accepts the attacks of the enemy, anticipating higher levels to always have higher devils. We all face challenges, especially when we are growing, but these are often rooted in our own character and maturity and the character and maturity of those around us. Operating from this codebook can sabotage our growth by causing us to blame the consequence of our character on demonic attack or to attribute the misbehavior of others to something purely demonic, sabotaging our ability to assist in their growth and pull the gold out of their lives.

These dialects and codebooks are not all wrong. Each has elements that are true, but most are centered around a particular belief or experience, one that may not be entirely accurate.

Here's a practical example of how this works in normal everyday language: One day, not long after my wife and I were married, she walked in the door and sat at the kitchen table. I was sitting on the couch and let out a heavy sigh.

"What?" she asked, snapping around to look at me.

"What about what?" I said, thrown off by her sudden response.

"Just what?!" She was getting more exasperated.

I had the sudden impression that I'd just wandered into a roomful of open bear traps. "Uh...I don't know."

"What are you mad about?"

"I'm not mad."

"Yes, you are."

This went on a bit longer than is necessary to convey here, but eventually we sleuthed out the solution. When my wife was growing up, her father would breathe heavily out of his nose when he was upset about something. This little piece of language had developed into a codebook that made it seem like my sigh was a sign that I was angry. This language was so strongly rooted in my wife's mind that it was hard for her to believe I wasn't angry, even when I told her otherwise.

Codebooks are powerful things. Imagine for a second that you burned your hand by resting it on a red-hot pan. If you do not have the context provided by culture and history, it is easy to imagine how you could develop wild misconceptions about the experience. You could assume that anything that is that particular shade of bright orangey red is dangerous and avoid all orange and red things for the rest of your life. You could assume that the pan was the problem and steer clear of all pots and pans. You could assume that the pain was a punishment for something you had done earlier that day.

These examples are silly, I know, but it is important to recognize that they are only silly because you already have the cultural and historical understanding that makes the reason for your hypothetically burnt hand clear. Without a clear understanding and a wealth of personal experience with the history and culture of heaven, the assumptions we make about the spirit realm are just as silly.

I believe the reason I suffered demonic attack for so long is simple: I had a spiritual codebook that allowed for it. It was subtle, and it was not intentional, but it was there, and I have shared it with you already. I believed that either I was losing my mind or the devil had decided to ruin my life.

This simple piece of belief was the open door. Something demonic introduced fear into my life, and I believed that it was allowed to.

Belief is a funny thing. We often think of it as something we do on purpose, and this is true of some beliefs, but most of them are far subtler than that. Every night I experienced fear and saw terrible things. I don't remember if it took a week, a month, or a year, but eventually my experience with fear created a codebook: I am either losing my mind or the devil has decided to ruin my life. I knew biblical truth that was the antidote for this belief, but my experience was speaking to me louder than the truth. I needed experience to change my belief. I needed experience to even realize that I was operating out of a belief.

Moving to a new church and learning about the prophetic gift caused a series of experiences that changed my codebook. I learned that God wanted to talk to me, a tangible and personal experience with His love. I told my parents what was happening, a healing release of the acceptance and comfort I was denying myself by hiding my pain. I spoke with leaders about what was going on and learned about a gift, an empowering understanding of identity and purpose. This made room for a new belief, a new spiritual dialect, and a revised codebook. Maybe I have a gift that I haven't learned how to use properly yet. And this new codebook completely changed my experience.

This is just one example of how profoundly our spiritual dialect and codebooks can affect our understanding of the spirit realm. This is why we are pursuing the language of heaven. We do not want a dialect that is based on a carnal, human perspective. We certainly don't want a dialect that is based on a demonic perspective. Instead we must humbly, patiently, and consistently pursue the perspective of heaven. It is the only way we will ever understand its language.

Learning the language of heaven is a lifelong endeavor. To learn it well, learn it accurately, and recognize where our preconceptions and misconceptions steer us wrong, we need to immerse ourselves in the culture and history of heaven. All language is learned best by immersing yourself in the culture the language comes from. It's the only way to discover all the little nuances you can't find in a dictionary.

The rest of this book will be an exercise in immersion. I'm going to share stories about seeing in the spirit realm and take time to discuss a few nuances of language, while trying to paint a broader and deeper picture of how it all works together. Please do not just read through these stories and take them at face value; look for the language.

Two more quick things before we dive in:

1. Understanding the language of heaven is best pursued with full immersion, and this book is not nearly enough. A hundred books would not be enough. You need people around you who are learning this language too, a whole community of them. Humankind has not been designed for isolation. If you read this book and then go off and try to figure the rest of it out for yourself, I guarantee you will end up with an inaccurate codebook. We need the friction of relationship to remove the jagged parts of our lives. Learning the language of heaven is no exception.

2. You need a relationship with the Bible. This isn't a finger-wagging, "You should be reading your Bible, sonny" message. In fact I think reading the Bible purely out of obligation is often a detriment to learning the language of heaven. But

you need to know the history and the
culture of the language you are learning,
and there's no other place where you'll
find more of it. I know not everyone is
built to be a scholar, but I do think all
of us have the responsibility to engage
with the level of scholarship we are
designed for and receive from those
who are gifted in this area.

All right, jumping off the soapbox and kicking it
into the bushes, let's go walking through this garden.

Oh yeah, one more thing: For those of you who
have read my previous books, you may notice that
some of these stories are repeats from those writings.
This is because some of those stories have very helpful
examples of the language of heaven, and the goals
of this book are better achieved with their inclusion.
Though you may be familiar with them, I encourage
you to still read through them. You will understand
them differently in this framework of understanding
the language of God. I have also adapted them with
additional details or more information about how
I understood them at the time. It is, unfortunately,
impractical to include every detail about the things I
see. This is a reality that has always bothered me, so
I am excited to have the opportunity to add dimen-
sion to these stories.

CHAPTER 3

PARKS AND RECREATION

YESTERDAY MORNING, I decided to exercise. There's a park near my house with a walking path around a small lake, which seemed like as good a place as any to start a lifelong journey toward total physical fitness. I dug out my unused running shoes, threw on some very used basketball shorts, found an uplifting exercise playlist, and drove down to the park.

It started out as a run, then slowed into a jog that deteriorated into a walk, all before my first lap around the lake. I spent a few minutes in self-loathing contemplation, feeling the flame of inspiration that had led to this morning's life-changing decision flicker and die in my heart. I was just starting to wonder if there were any ice cream shops that opened at 8:15 in the morning when a woman ran past me.

She was your typical jogger: ponytail, black tank top with matching tights and headband. Her angel was running in perfect step alongside her, wearing a black tracksuit. The angel looked almost just like the woman she was running with: same hair, same height, similar face. I would have thought it was her twin sister if she weren't partially transparent and running on the air as often as she ran on the ground.

Every few minutes the angel would jump and skip in a little orbit around the woman, waving her arms wildly and shouting encouragement. I couldn't hear what the angel was saying or read its lips, but everything about her expression was enthused with unreserved and sincere joy.

A few moments later a man ran by me. He was as fit as could be. His muscles had muscles. He looked how I expected to look after two or three weeks of working out when I started my fitness journey earlier that morning. A demon was chasing after him. It was ashy gray with long, bony legs, and was poking at the man's back with a long iron prod.

The man's angel flew past my ear, golden wings arched back, a shining sword in his hand. It struck out at the demon, knocking the iron prod off-balance.

The demon threw a shoulder into the angel, knocking it to the ground. The angel landed hard, rolled, then sprung forward without hesitation, shouldering the demon in return. This only caused the demon to stumble slightly. The battle continued as the man made his way around the lake and passed me again. The angel attacked tirelessly, but nothing stopped the demon from prodding the man for more than a second or two.

The woman and the man finished their run a few seconds apart; this appeared to be a coincidence, since they didn't speak and walked to separate cars. The woman's angel continued shouting encouragement at her person, rubbing her shoulders and back as she slowed to a stop.

The demon dropped the prod as the man stopped at his car and pulled a bottle of water from a cooler in his trunk. The demon pressed blood-red lips against the man's ear, hissing and spitting so virulently that it worked up foam at the corner of its mouth. Again, I couldn't hear what the demon was saying, but every word looked punctuated and profane.

The angel doubled its effort, swinging at the demon with heavy two-handed strokes, but these glanced off as if the demon's skin were made of thick steel. The angel's blows fell so hard that his sword began to bend and crumple. It soon became so misshapen that he threw it aside and began pounding at the demon with bare fists, but still this did nothing.

The angel was strong, even more muscular than the man he was trying to protect, yet still his strikes did nothing as the demon spit furious words into the man's ear. The man showed no significant expression. He stared into the distance, sipping his water and wiping the sweat from his chest with a towel.

A look of desperation came over the angel's face as he shifted from throwing ineffective blows to grasping at the demon in an eager attempt to peel him away from the man. But, as though the demon were covered in grease, the angel couldn't seem to get a grip anywhere.

Then a phone rang.

The man reached into the trunk, looked at the phone, sighed, and then answered. The moment he looked at the phone, the demon's persistent flow of violent words suddenly halted. Half a heartbeat later the angel found a grip on the demon and yanked it backward in a full-on suplex. The demon slammed into the concrete in a bone-crumpling heap. The angel showed the same lack of hesitation it had displayed during the man's run; it leapt forward and kicked the demon in the side, sending it fifteen feet across the parking lot. The angel rushed forward again, thrust by its powerful golden wings, and picked the demon up. The angel carried it high into the air, knocked it around a few times in a brief one-person game of aerial ping-pong, and then pelted it with a mighty kick beyond the edge of the horizon.

The man continued his phone call, still completely unaware.

Here we have two people doing more or less the same thing: going for a jog. Yet in the spirit, something radically different was happening. The woman was being encouraged by her personal angel. Oh, right... personal angels; we haven't talked about them yet.

Every person I have ever met has a personal angel, an angel that is assigned specifically to them for their entire life. Some people call them guardian angels, but they do a lot more than guard you. They pray for you, encourage you, worship God alongside you, minister to you, and fight off demons that are trying to poke you while you're out for a jog. That's why I call them personal angels. Is it the right name for them? I don't know, but it's what I call them.

Anyway, the woman was being encouraged by her personal angel. The man was being attacked by a demon while his angel struggled to fend it off. Let's lay these pieces out on the table and take a good look at them. Again, we must remember that we are not just trying to figure out what this series of events means; we are learning a language. To help with this, I want to walk you through what I was thinking when I saw these events unfold.

First, I saw the angel running alongside the woman. She matched her stride, was wearing an outfit that went along with what the woman was wearing, and looked very similar to her. You may think these details are what made it clear that this was her angel, but that's not so. Sometimes people's personal angels look just like them; sometimes they look radically different. Sometimes they match their person in demeanor and temperament, and sometimes they are the exact opposite. Despite this, even in a room of a hundred people, I can almost always instantly recognize which angel goes with which person.

It's hard to point at any one detail that makes this possible because it seems to be the result of a thousand tiny details. Their attention, posture, and movement are all oriented around their person in a way that shows a rich form of deference and care. None of these comparisons are quite right, but it is somewhat similar to the way newly married couples posture themselves toward one another in public, or the way a toddler orients himself or herself in a room based on where his or her mother is standing. It's hard to say exactly how you can tell that these things belong together, but it is also undeniable. This is how it is with personal angels.

That this woman's angel was encouraging her was not surprising; I see angels doing this all the time. What stood out to me was that she seemed to be specifically excited about the fact that she was running.

I've never really thought of exercise as a particularly spiritual activity. I mean, sure, it is in that "All things unto the Lord" sort of way. But is the activity itself spiritual? If so, is it spiritual because it's good for your body and healthy choices are good spiritual choices? Maybe. But that feels like an overly forced piece of logic. Is it only spiritual if it's being done "unto the Lord"? If so, how do you make sure you're doing it unto the Lord? Do you pray while you're doing it? Do you make sure to end your run by saying, "I want to thank my Lord and Savior, Jesus Christ," like they do at the end of a football game?

I didn't have any great answers to any of these questions, and it seemed like each was missing some part of the point, but the man ran past me before I had time to think it the rest of the way through.

I see demons attack people all the time. Hearing this usually freaks people out, but it's really not that big a deal. I think it scares people because most of us have a perspective about demons that was formed by a bad experience in our past, a bad experience we hear about from someone else, or movies. That last one might seem silly, but it has a much bigger effect than you might think. The number of people who went to therapists and pastors because they thought they were possessed by a demon skyrocketed when the film *The*

Exorcist was released. Whenever a similarly themed movie gains popularity, there is a similar bump in reported demonic attacks. I'm not saying these movies are causing demonic attacks in a direct sense (demons jumping out of the screen and whatnot), but they influence our belief system. If we believe that demons can attack us, then they will be more than happy to do whatever they can to reinforce that belief system.

In my experience, demonic attack is much more mundane than horror films would have you believe. Most of what demons do is try to get you to believe lies. They usually choose lies that suit our circumstances. No one will ever love you. You are worthless. God doesn't care about you. You'll never be satisfied. They find the lie that sticks to your history and circumstances and then keep pressing on it until it integrates itself into your view of the world, becoming part of your lens.

I see demons attack people all the time. Sometimes it's subtle. Sometimes it's aggressive.

I don't know what lie the demon with the iron prod was telling the man as he ran, but I could tell that he was believing it. The prod tells me that the demon was trying to motivate him, to drive him. Maybe he was told he was too wimpy or ugly when he was young and getting fit was a way to compensate for that feeling of inadequacy. Maybe he was having relational struggles and needed to feel the confidence and control of doing something that he knew how to do well. Maybe he was just angry about something and needed to let out some aggression. Whatever it was, the demon was trying to use it as an opportunity to reinforce a lie.

Does this mean that for this man, going for a run was wrong or bad? Not necessarily. Earlier I talked about how I was feeling defeated when I went out to run. I said it jokingly, but I really did think about getting ice cream. Was a demon telling me to get ice cream? Would it have been a sin to go get ice cream? Not necessarily. Jogging and ice cream are not inherently good or bad (though I must say that in my heart, jogging is bad and ice cream is good), but using anything as a coping mechanism rather than working on the underlying problem often leads to bad.

I don't know this man's story, but I could confidently guess that the demon was using whatever opportunity his life circumstances had presented to try to reinforce unhealthy patterns of coping. I'm guessing the run did not solve whatever struggle he was going through. This is when the demon leaned in and started spitting whatever lie would suit that moment of vulnerability. This is what demons do.

Now, you might be wondering, why couldn't the angel just chop the demon's head off or something? We'll discuss this in more detail down the line, but for now let's just establish that if you want to understand the language of heaven, then you will need to grow adept at understanding the relationship between literalism and metaphor.

If we get overly literal in the interpretation of what we see in the spirit, then we could interpret the scene with the jogging man, the demon, and the angel to mean that the demon was more powerful than the angel and it had to struggle mightily to overcome it. The angel was knocked away by the demon repeatedly during the jog. All the angel's attacks barely knocked the demon off-balance, as if there were a hundred-pound difference between them. Was the demon more powerful than the angel? That doesn't seem right—but then why did it look that way?

If we look at the whole story and add a bit of context, it becomes clear that this was not just a picture of the struggle between heaven and hell; it was a picture of the struggle between heaven and hell within the heart of a man.

I see demons attack people all the time. In church, during worship, while people are praying for them, as they are reading the Bible—I see it all the time. Does this mean that demons are more powerful than angels and the presence of God? Does this mean that hell is more powerful than heaven? Nope. It means that our choices and beliefs determine how much heaven or how much hell we live in.

I have seen demons scrabbling like a rat in a trap,

desperately trying to get away from a person they are attached to because the presence of God was so thick in a room, yet they were stuck because of the person's belief. Their belief in the lie was so strong that not even the demon could flee.

I don't know what lie this man was believing, but I know that he was believing a lie. That angel threw himself at the demon with the passion and fury of a parent rescuing his child from an attacking dog. There was sweat pouring from every part of his body. Tears were streaming from both eyes as he beat his sword to pieces over the demon's back. Genuine desperation was written on his face as he struggled to get a grip on the demon, and there was pure wrath in every movement as he kicked and punched the demon out of sight.

The angel flew back down after the demon was gone. I don't know what expression I expected to see on his face. Maybe frustration: "How could you believe a lie like that?" Maybe disappointment: "You can't let yourself get fooled that way." But his expression said none of these things.

Instead, he landed right next to the man, wrapped his arms around him in a big bear hug, with an expression of exhausted satisfaction that spoke more clearly than words, "We did it. We got him. Great job." I'm sure many of us have learned to expect disappointment and judgment when we fail. Personal angels, each of whom has been present for every one of any given person's worst moments, rarely respond this way. This is not to say they do not lament the destruction and pain caused by patterns of sin, no matter how big or small. It just means that they couch their sorrow in unrelenting belief, causing them to respond to our failings with purest hope.

I don't know who called the man or what they said, but I know it was who he needed to talk to. It broke whatever cycle of belief the demon was reinforcing, giving the angel the authority to remove it completely.

It might be surprising or even hard to believe that jogging is such a profoundly spiritual activity, but that's where we need to continue to adjust our codebook: everything is a spiritual activity; you are a spirit. Everything you do has spiritual consequence. Everything you think has spiritual consequence. Everything you believe has spiritual consequence.

The story above is only a very small part of what I saw that day. There were angels dancing in and around the park, skipping across the lake and through the trees. They were worshipping God and partnering with the beauty of nature, which glorifies Him simply by existing. There were half a dozen angels playing with a group of kids in a nearby field, investing in their identity, fending off the early seeds of lies. There were seven other people who came and went, jogging or walking, as I made my way around the lake. They each had things going on in the spirit around them just as complex and unique as the woman and the man in the story above.

It may seem strange to think of jogging as a spiritual activity, but again, the reality is that everything is a spiritual activity. All sports, all leisure, all hobbies— they all carry spiritual weight. Not only do they carry inherent spiritual meaning, but I believe that all these things can have meaning for the kingdom of God.

A week later my family and I went to visit the park again. I had decided to retire undefeated from my running career, so I took the kids to the playground while my wife went for a run.

There are many things that my wife, April, is good at, but one of the things she *is* is a runner. I don't know this because of her successful running career in high school and college. I don't know this because of how often she runs. I know this because when she runs, I see glory.

She started near the playground, giving me and the kids a smile and a wave before starting off. Her angel looks like she usually does when April goes for a run: pink headband, pink running shorts, pink running shoes. April almost never wears pink, but her angel almost always does. They ran off together, slowly at first, finding the rhythm. I turned to play with the kids, doing my best to balance being fun and making sure no one fell off the monkey bars.

I felt it happen before I saw it. Maybe it's because you're more in tune with the gifts of the people you love, or maybe it's because this gift of April's is particularly special. A pressure ran through my chest, and I turned to see a sight I had seen many times before.

April was halfway through her first lap, and glory was following behind her. It flicked off the back of her hair as she ran, a wake of sunset and fireflies, a stream of widening light that hung in the air like sunshine in the clouds. Her angel ran beside her, bopping up and down in perfect rhythm. She no longer wore a pink running outfit. She wore a long, flowing dress made of the wind itself.

You may not have much of a tolerance for this kind of saccharine metaphor, but saying it any other way is less true. April left the sunset in her wake, and her angel wore the wind.

There had been nearly a dozen angels dancing across the lake this time, worshipping alongside nature. They were waving and swirling long streamers through the water. As soon as the glory appeared, they all leapt into step behind April and her angel, dancing through the light and wind, using their streamers and hands to make patterns in the air. They were worshipping God.

It suddenly occurred to me that April's running was worship the same way that a lake is worship, the same way a field of flowers is worship, the same way a snow-covered mountain is worship. It is worship because it is beautiful, and beauty belongs to God.

I don't know how to tell you to do something "unto the glory of God," but I know what it looks like.

CHAPTER 4

THEIR ONLY JOB

I'VE BEEN SEEING personal angels my whole life. Like I said earlier, I've never met anyone without one, and in case you haven't noticed, there are a lot of people around. Despite these being some of the most common kinds of angels I see, I always had the hardest time explaining what they do. Worship angels partner with worship. Protection angels partner with God's protection over us. Personal angels worship alongside us, defend us from the attacks of the enemy, encourage us, partner with God's purposes in our lives... It always sounds like an arbitrary list of tasks. It's one of the reasons I call them personal angels. I saw them a bit like supernatural personal assistants.

Furthermore, I didn't exactly understand what the point of a personal angel was. Don't get me wrong; I appreciate them being there. But what is their purpose? As Christians, we all have the Holy Spirit within us. God makes Himself present in our lives, and we can speak to Him directly. What extra benefit does a personal angel provide?

Eventually I realized the reason I had such a hard time defining what a personal angel did was because of a little piece of God's nature that I forgot to consider, almost like forgetting a bit of grammar when trying to form a coherent sentence.

April and I had been married for a little more than a year. We always wanted to have kids, but our conversations were starting to sound less like dreams and more like plans. We were going to wait until we were married for two years, but we wanted a big family and April was concerned that her running career might make it hard for her to get pregnant.

We were sitting on the couch in our apartment when we made the decision. We were going to start trying to get pregnant. The moment we agreed on this, an angel stepped into the room. She was the same height as April, had brown hair and pleasant blue eyes, and was wearing a classic nurse's uniform, something straight out of a World War II movie, hair in a bun, little white hat with a red cross, the whole thing. I knew April had some concerns about getting pregnant, so I figured this was some kind of health or nurse angel sent to take care of her.

The angel followed April everywhere she went for the three months we spent trying to get pregnant. It jumped up and down with joy along with us when we got our first positive pregnancy test. I would often see the nurse angel rubbing April's growing belly with a soft cloth, running comforting fingers through her hair as she went through horrible bouts of morning sickness (more like morning, noon, and night sickness), and massaging her back as the growing baby put more and more strain on her body.

The nurse angel followed April all the way up to the big day. It was standing with her when her water broke. It rode with us to the hospital. It was in the room during every moment of labor. And it was there the moment my son was born.

My son lay on April's chest for a moment that seemed as close to a second as it did to an hour. Eventually it was time for the doctor to check on April and the baby to go to the baby inspection table (it probably has a fancier name). I followed the baby and noticed that the nurse angel followed along right behind me. I stood there for a moment, feeling worlds of love open in parts of my heart I'd never felt before. The nurse angel stood right beside me, staring just as intently as I was.

The nurse angel followed me as I escorted my son from room to room for all the baby tests. It stood right next to the little crib as I called my grandfather to tell him that we had decided to name the baby after him, Haydon. It followed my son everywhere, never letting more than a step or two of space come between them for the rest of the day.

Later that night, April lay in the hospital bed, fast asleep, while Haydon slept soundly in the tiny hospital crib. The futon I was sleeping on seemed specially designed for causing lasting back problems, so I was having a hard time falling asleep—that and I was incredibly excited.

I kept staring at my sleeping son, feeling a love like none I had ever experienced grow larger with every passing second. It was then I noticed the nurse angel looking down at Haydon from the other side of the crib. The nurse outfit was gone, the brown hair was hanging loose over her shoulders, and she was wearing a simple blue tunic. She looked younger now too, but I knew it was still her. She had the same face, and her eyes were the same too.

Those eyes were looking down at my son with absolute affection. I recognized the look. It perfectly reflected the same overwhelming love I was feeling. I am sure the angel's expression matched my own. It was the one I had when I looked at my newborn son. It was the one I had when I looked at April. It was the look of love, the kind of love that can only happen between those who belong together.

Most of you have probably already guessed where this is going, but it was a complete surprise to me at the time. I looked up at the angel and said, "You're not a pregnancy angel or a nurse angel. You're his angel, aren't you?" tilting my head toward Haydon.

The angel looked up to meet my gaze, smiled, and then nodded, tipping her head with a little "well duh" attitude.

That question I had rolled around in my head so many times before came rushing back into my mind. What is the purpose of a personal angel? What is the point? What is their job?

Haydon's angel looked at me, smiled again, and then answered.

When I hear angels speak, it's rarely an English sentence. I see their mouths move and I sometimes hear a sound, but it bears no resemblance to any dialect I've ever heard on earth. Rather than hearing words, blocks of information just land in my head; I suddenly just know what they are saying. It's something between a download of data and the feeling of recognizing whether a series of notes are intended to evoke sadness or joy. It isn't either of these things, but it is like them. Since I hear this way, I can usually translate what I heard into an English sentence, but if I'm being honest, it always feels as if something is lost in the translation—like hearing poetry in a language it wasn't written in;

the meaning is there but something precious is inevitably lost.

I've tried to say what Haydon's angel told me a hundred different ways, but all of them fall short of how it sounded in my heart. Here's attempt one hundred and one: I wondered again about the purpose of personal angels. Haydon's angel looked up at me, smiled, and said, "What's wrong with the idea that the Father saw fit to send someone whose only job is to love you every day of your life?"

If we want to understand the spirit realm by learning the language of heaven, then we must recognize that love is its chief rule of grammar.

Personal angels do a lot of things for us. They pray for us, guard us, and support us—but these are not their purpose. Personal angels exist because God wanted every person on this planet to have someone whose sole purpose is to love them well. Everything they do is an expression of this.

I have five children now, and I can tell you that each of their angels showed up the moment April and I decided it was time to start trying to have a new baby. Each one followed April in the months we tried to get pregnant, throughout her pregnancy, and during every step of her labor, and then left to follow our newborn baby.

I've never met anyone without a personal angel, no matter who they were, no matter what they were doing. I've never seen them judge the person they are with. I've never seen them be disappointed. I have seen them hurt, though, all the time. But like a mother, like a brother, like a devoted friend, their pain is the kind that can only come out of unconditional love toward an imperfect person.

God's love is vast and mysterious. Every experience you have ever had with the meaning of that word is a small and incomplete picture of that endless mystery. We would all do well to remember that no matter how much we have learned of it, we do not understand it yet, and maybe we never will. But we can learn about it more every day.

CHAPTER 5

THE BUSINESS OF GARDENING

WHAT DOES IT mean for everything to be spiritual? It means that every thought, action, reaction, and circumstance between them has spiritual consequence. Everything is affected by the spirit, and the spirit affects everything.

At first this may seem overwhelming or hard to believe. It might give you the feeling of walking through an antique shop, with all God's plans and purposes laid out like delicate and expensive vases. One wrong move and you send everything crashing to the floor. If you have a more fearful perspective of the spirit realm, then it may seem like walking down a dark forest full of angry demons ready to snap at the first sign of weakness.

While there is some truth to these metaphors, they both come from a very powerless perspective. Paying attention to what is happening in the spirit realm may be a new concept for you, but trust me, you are already way more aware of what is happening in the spirit than you think. Remember, you are a spirit. Whether you've known it or not, you have been living in the spirit realm for your whole life.

Rather than an antique shop full of breakables or a dark forest full of monsters, I think it is best for us to think of the spirit realm as a garden. Everything you say, think, and do affects the garden around you. Some thoughts are like the seeds of fruit-bearing plants; they germinate and grow into thriving things that provide ongoing nutrition to you and those around you. Some thoughts are like weeds; they suck the life out of everything around them and provide nothing of value. Some thoughts are like water; they refresh us and anyone we share them with. Some thoughts are like poison; they wreak havoc and damage the soil.

If we think of our interaction with the spirit realm this way, it is easy to imagine all our thoughts, words, and actions spreading out into the spirit like seeds, water, and sunshine, affecting us and the lives of others well beyond us.

When I walk into a house where people spend a lot of time in prayer and worship, I can see it. Thick, healthy vines covered in green leaves and blooming flowers grow along the walls. Flowing water springs up from fountains or natural springs in every room. Angels move around the house, tending to each thriving plant. In the same way that the weather system of a rain forest allows for a tremendous variety of plant and animal life, a home where people live a lifestyle of prayer and worship creates a weather system where a vibrant spiritual garden can grow.

In the same way, a home where there is an abundance of anxiety, stress, and anger creates a different kind of garden. Sharp rocks grow up from the ground like stalagmites, each with jagged, cutting edges. Dry grass covers the ground, thorny weeds abound, and good seeds remain dormant on the cracked soil.

Most places I visit are not so binary. Every home, like every family, has strengths and weaknesses. I have seen a house that had one of the richest worship environments, and the walls were absolutely covered in gorgeously healthy plant life. Though the walls and ceiling were covered with multicolored leaves and flowers, the ground was bone dry. It was a home that valued an emphasis on spiritual things but lacked the groundedness and roots for healthy relational connectedness.

Another time, I visited a house that was littered with sharp rocks, signs of a cutting, sarcastic, and angry environment. Despite this, thick-rooted plants made their way around the rocks and into the rich, dark soil; a sign that, regardless of what dysfunction they had, this was a family that had still managed to remain connected to each other.

It isn't just our homes that look this way. Businesses, schools, parks, towns, cities, counties, and nations— they are all part of a vast spiritual garden, growing based on the actions, thoughts, and beliefs of the people within them. Everything we do has spiritual consequences. Everything makes room for more of the seeds of heaven or the consuming destruction of the enemy. In the grand scheme of things, any one action or belief has little consequence, but everything contributes to the grand ecosystem of the spirit.

While I was writing this book, three friends of mine started new businesses. I took the opportunity to watch what happened in the spirit around each of them for their first few years of business, curious how each of their approaches would affect them spiritually. These aren't their real names, but this is what happened with them.

First up is Dom. Dom is your classic ideas man. In the years I've known him, he's had seven different jobs, started nine different businesses, moved six times, and had seventy ideas for new businesses since breakfast this morning. He is caring, kind, and idealistic, and he loves Jesus with his whole heart. Though his ideas often sound great in concept, none have come to any great success.

Dom's latest idea was a new entrepreneurial philanthropic venture designed to make large amounts of money for investors and provide healthy water to those who do not have access to it. I saw great sparks of light flying off him as he shared the details of the venture and how it will impact those in need around the world. The sparks grew out from him into long, twisting, red-hot strips of molten metal, like the shavings in an iron works.

The more he spoke, the more the strips of hot metal erupted from him. They came so fast and furious that they bunched up and tangled on the ground.

After a few minutes, two angels appeared to gather up the pieces of glowing metal, as well as the others that came flying out from Dom as he continued to share his vision for the business. Most of the metal had become so entangled that the angels had to pick it up in knotted clumps.

I felt excited by his idea, but his history of false starts and overambition made me feel nervous for him. The metal that was coming out as he spoke was real, though. By that I mean it had substance. If his idea was truly an empty one, I would see smoke, vapor, or something else insubstantial. Ideas from God come with the spiritual resources to accomplish them, they have substance, and the metal that appeared was evidence that Dom's idea was being supported by heaven.

I couldn't help but notice, however, that while Dom's excited description of his life-changing business continued to produce more and more strips of this superheated heavenly metal, the angels each wore a patiently confused expression. They faithfully picked up each strip but then stood idly, almost as if they didn't know what to do with it. They just stood there with armfuls of metal strips that seemed to get more tangled by the second. And as Dom continued to speak, the metal started to cool.

Next up is Will. Will is the youngest of the three businesspeople in our story. He attended a prestigious school, graduated with several good job opportunities, and decided to work with the family business for a few years to gain some experience. His new business is tech oriented, and though it sounds neat, I still don't think I understand it well enough to describe it as anything other than "tech stuff."

Will is a very spiritual man. He loves Jesus and lives his life with an almost monk-like spiritual orientation. He wakes up early each morning to pray and study the Bible for at least an hour. He spends at least another hour in silent contemplation. Then he goes out for a jog while listening to an audiobook about ancient Hebrew theology.

An angel in white robes stood just behind him on the day he first told me about his new business. I did my best to understand what he intended for his new company to do, but after asking three separate times, "So what exactly are you doing again?" I gave up and just watched what the angel was doing.

With each calm and detailed sentence of incomprehensible description, the angel set a small scene in the air just above my friend's head. Like a painter, the angel waved one hand in the air, leaving a small flowing waterfall in its trail. It tapped closed fingers here and there, leaving bright yellow flowers in each place. It rubbed in some leafy greens and created a little pond where the waterfall landed.

Over the course of his description the angel painted a small garden into existence just behind my friend.

"I guess what I'm trying to do," my friend said with emphasis that pulled me from my distraction, "is to create something that fulfills a need in an easier way that is a benefit to customers, a benefit to me, and makes space for a business that is beneficial to work at."

With this, the angel set a little dollop of sunlight just at the corner of the small garden, casting the whole scene in sunset light that made every element overflow with beauty.

I still didn't know exactly what kind of business my friend was starting, but I was very curious to see how that little garden would manifest itself through his business.

Person number three is Jack. Jack is a salt-of-the-earth entrepreneur. He has started, grown, and sold several businesses already. All of these were blue-collar sorts of businesses—landscaping, construction, and that kind of thing. The economic landscape in the fields Jack had been working in had shifted the last few years, causing his last two ventures to be false starts. Jack was smart, though. He saw what was happening before investing too heavily and pulled the plug before he lost much.

Those experiences led Jack to feel more uncertain than he had in a long time. He usually could just see what needed to be done and do it. He took some extra time to spend time with God, go on long walks, and speak with some mentors.

After taking some time to rethink his approach, Jack shared his new idea with me. It was still connected to the fields he knew well, but it was an area in which he had never worked before, so he was still a bit uncertain.

As he spoke, angels carried in gigantic wooden crates. Some were big enough to hold a car, others were long and flat, and some were no bigger than a shoebox. By the time Jack was done telling me about the business, he was surrounded by ten yards of crates in all different sizes.

I have seen this kind of thing several times before. Some people have a gift for building things. They know how to put a team together, they have a vision for what needs to be done, and they see the steps to get there. Whenever a builder talks to me about something they are building, I see heaven deliver materials. Does this mean that everything these people do is flawlessly successful? Nope. But it does mean that even when their plans fail, they learn from the experience and apply the lesson to the next idea.

Seeing this made me feel confident that Jack's new business was going to thrive.

I chatted with Dom off and on about how his new water business was going. He got meetings with investors, had prototypes built, and assembled a small team to help develop the project and get the word out. I saw the angels with him each time, and each time they were carrying the tangled-up pieces of metal. They had long since cooled, but whenever Dom talked about his passion for the project, they started to heat up again. The investors were always interested, and the team was always motivated—at least Dom said that they were.

Anytime he talked about the details of the business, the angels would pull and twist the knotted metal, trying to untangle it. Usually this looked like a fruitless effort. The metal only ended up tangled in a different way than it had been before. Sometimes, when

Dom was showing his passion for the idea and the metal started to heat up, it looked like the angels were starting to make some headway on separating the pieces. Usually, however, by the time I saw him next, the metal was just as tangled as it had been at the start.

For months I heard about how Dom was just a meeting or two from breakthrough. Investors fell through. Team members quit. New investors accepted meetings. New team members joined. Tangle. Untangle. Tangled again.

Will spent months and months setting up his business. He worked with multiple developers to build software. He ran tests with several friends and family members as pretend clients. He pulled in multiple friends and mentors to get input on how to construct the business better.

Each time he shared about this process with me, I saw the angel working on the garden behind him. It adjusted the way the flowers lay, it shifted the flow of the waterfall, it shaped and reshaped the pond; each shift made it even more beautiful.

Will prayed about every decision he made, continued his lifestyle of spending long hours with the Lord on a regular basis, and tried to read every book about business written by a Christian.

After a very long process of preparation, the day finally came for Will to launch his business. Though I was still unsure what he was actually selling, I was excited for him. Things started slowly, but bit by bit, month by month, Will's business continued to grow. He was soon able to hire a few employees and take some time to set up plans for how to expand things for the future.

Several months after Will launched his business, he was contacted by his aunt. Her son had just dropped out of college to pursue a career on YouTube, much to the horror of her and her husband. After much bickering, they had decided to allow him to still live at the house and pursue his new career, but only if he was willing to take on another job in the meantime. Her son had a spotty record with some of his previous jobs, so she thought that Will's company would be the perfect opportunity for him to learn how to be a model employee.

Will was hesitant, but he also had a very strong value for family. It seemed wrong to say no. When Will told me about his cousin coming to work for him and the reservations he had about it, I saw a big, gray toad leap into the middle of his pristine garden.

Jack's business was thriving from the start. Despite it being a new field for him, he quickly gained a reputation for being one of the most honest and excellent companies in the area. Within just a few months he had more customers than he could manage on his own. He took time to train each new employee on how to maintain the level of quality and detail his company was known for. He worked with a marketing company to develop a company brand and spread the word about his business as widely as possible.

Whenever Jack told me about how his business was going, I saw teams of angels opening the wooden crates that surrounded him. Inside there was a wide variety of construction materials; everything from structural components like steel beams, long timbers, and metal bolts to more decorative elements like statues, ornately carved siding, and finely crafted lighting fixtures. It looked like everything that would be needed to build an immaculate estate.

My first impression, if I'm being honest, was a negative one. I'm not much of a businessperson. I'm fonder of writing, art, and creativity—all things that, in my mind, are often confined by the limits imposed on them by business. Though it was not an opinion I had formed with much intention, I tended to think that most business was just a well-organized excuse for exploitation and greed. So when I saw all the fancy decorative elements that were coming out of Jack's boxes, I thought, "Wow, what a wonderful empire you're building for yourself."

Despite the hindrance of my punk-rock-tinged prejudice, I knew that nothing that came from heaven could be bad. While I'm sure that some people use what God has intended for good for their own personal gain, or even to harm others, it was easy to see that Jack was not that kind of person.

Every conversation I had with Jack about business would inevitably end up being about the kingdom of God being perpetuated through business. It wasn't just about businessmen making money to give to the church and to missionaries; it was far deeper than that. Jack had a vision for thousands of businesses, all built on kingdom values—not just companies that include an ichthus (the Christian fish symbol) in their logo, but places that spread the kingdom through the way they treat and train their employees, how they serve their customers and community, and the kingdom excellence they show in every facet of their operation.

I remember one of the first times Jack told me about this idea. An angel had been moving a large statue out of a crate just behind him. As Jack went on, talking about how companies that are built on kingdom values transform communities, the angel gently set the statue on the ground. Almost immediately, a thick patch of green grass spread out across the ground from where the statue rested. It slowly covered the entire floor of the room we were standing in; then it began to blossom with delicate purple flowers and then fruiting trees.

Though I still have a hard time not being distracted by the harm that greed has caused through business, Jack helped me see that business itself is intended to be a tool in the hands of God. Every time I have seen Jack or one of his workers, I have seen that lush garden. It fills the room when they have a staff meeting together. It lingers at any site they've worked at. Jack is a wonderful example of how everything affects the spirit realm. Every bill he sends, every correction he gives to an employee, every response to a crisis or mistake, every aspect of every job is an opportunity to release a seed of the kingdom.

Dom did his best to get his idea off the ground, but it never really did. Soon his team only consisted of his wife, his mother, and his two daughters. He no longer had any meetings on the calendar with potential investors. And his family was being overstrained by the financial and time investment.

The angels still carried the twisted-up tangles of metal whenever I saw him around. They were just as knotted up as they had been at the start, maybe more so.

Dom ended up taking a job at a privately owned manufacturing plant. The owner took a liking to him, took him under his wing, and started training him to be his second-in-command. Over the weeks and months at his new position, I still saw the same angels following Dom. The knots of metal grew tighter and tighter each time I saw them, until finally they had each condensed down into a tight ball.

I asked Dom if he had any hopes of revisiting his

water business in the future. Though I had done my best to ask it kindly, he gave a distinctly sheepish smile when he told me that he had decided to put it on the shelf. Maybe it was for a later day.

As he said this, the lumps of metal grew red hot in the angels' hands. Each angel kneaded its lump a few times, shaping it like a loaf of bread. They then each placed the reshaped metal somewhere behind Dom's back, just where it had come from when he had first shared his idea with me.

Will's cousin caused a series of problems all throughout his business. He didn't take the position very seriously at first. Will tried to give him feedback, but confrontation was never his strong suit. He let his cousin get away with slacking. This harmed the workflow in his small business and caused resentment from the other employees.

Every time Will talked about what was happening in his business, I'd see that fat, gray toad jumping all around his garden. It stomped on flowers, knocked over precisely placed stones, and kicked up mud in the water. The angel kept darting around, trying to snag the toad, but even the few times it managed to grab it, the toad slipped free.

The interpretation of this vision seemed obvious to me. Will's cousin was making a mess in Will's thoughtfully crafted business, just as the toad was making a mess in the otherwise serene garden. Does this mean that Will's cousin was a demon or being controlled by demons? That seems a bit overdramatic. Did this mean that his cousin was being used as a tool of the enemy to undermine Will's business? Though this may be part of the truth, I think this is a dangerously oversimplified approach that makes it far too easy to treat Will's cousin as the villain of this story.

Will's cousin had some character deficits, and Will had some character deficits. The collision of these deficits caused a conflict. The demonic was, as it almost always is, taking advantage of the friction between these two imperfect people.

I saw the little gray toad lash out with its tongue at Will's ear on several occasions. This always happened when Will was talking about how frustrated his cousin was making him. He had considered firing him on numerous occasions but always felt that the Lord was asking to keep him on. Was this a genuine word from the Lord or Will's value for family guiding him? I am still not sure.

I wish I could say that Will experienced some grand divine intervention that brought benevolent resolution to the situation with his cousin, but that's not what happened. Over several months of frustration, Will's company found a certain level of homeostasis. Will managed to get a little more direct with his cousin, though he never put strong boundaries on him. Will managed to pacify the frustrations of his other employees with a combination of extra compensation and increased flexibility in their work schedule. And Will's cousin found a spot in the company where he could be at least a bit helpful without dropping too many balls.

When I look at Will in the spirit, I still see the garden behind him. The angel has repaired all the damage the toad caused during its months-long rampage. The toad is still there, nestled in a little bundle of flowers next to the waterfall, not causing much trouble but not going away. Every now and again I see the toad flick out its tongue at Will's ear, trying to see if it can inject a little bitterness, maybe even a drop of resentment.

Jack's business continued to grow and thrive. He was invited to speak at several business events to share his heart for kingdom business. His employees continued to thrive under his leadership, not just as workers, but as people.

Despite this, the economic landscape has rumbled in many different directions these last few years. At the time of this writing, Jack's company is not doing very well. Jack needs to decide if this is a storm to be weathered or if the ever-shifting lands of commerce no longer have room for what he has created. He seeks the Lord about it regularly, thinks of the needs of his employees, and pulls on his own wisdom as well as the wisdom of those he has surrounded himself with.

I still see angels unloading crates around Jack. Despite the turmoil his company is in, he still carries a grace for business. This is true in heaven, even if some would not judge it to be so on earth. Some days, when he is talking about his passion for representing God's kingdom through business, his hands begin to glow. Streams of water fall from his fingertips, and thick patches of thriving garden spring up wherever it falls.

It doesn't seem fair. Jack is a kind and generous man. He is savvy in business and not afraid to pull on the strengths and talents of others. He is a lover of God and sees all of business through the filter of God's kingdom. Why should his business fail? Why should it even struggle? Why would it do anything other than thrive?

The initial temptation is to respond like Job's friends in the Bible and insist that Jack has some secret sin or character flaw that is causing harm to his business. This, however, comes from a codebook that insists that good things happen to good people and bad things happen to bad people. Is that the way God created the world to work? If so, then is having a perpetually thriving business what good looks like? I don't know the answers to these questions, and neither does Jack; I've asked him many times.

Whatever the case, and whatever happens to Jack's current business, something tells me that in another year or two or ten, Jack will be thriving in the spirit and on the earth, and he will be helping others to do the same.

———

There we have it: three lives over the course of more than a year, three businesses with varying levels of success, and three different kinds of spiritual impact.

While I want to leave plenty of room for you to draw your own conclusions, I do want to highlight a few things that stood out to me as I watched these three businessmen.

Dom is one of the most fun and charismatic people I know. He is brimming with ideas, and truthfully, many of them are very good. He just seems to lack the perspective, ability, or capacity (I don't know; maybe a business coach could tell me what it is) to make his ideas a reality.

The strips of metal that erupted out of him looked like raw materials. They were from heaven. They were good. But he did not have the tools, the team, or the know-how to take those raw materials and turn them into something useful.

Now that Dom is working with someone who believes in him but also has more wisdom and experience than he does, I hope that he takes the opportunity to recognize the shortcomings that have led so many of his ideas to fruitlessness. Though I am sure some part of him feels that he is selling out by taking a normal job, I think this may be the exact thing that grows him into the kind of person that makes dreams come true. I felt tremendous hope and the kindness of the Lord when I saw that the angels had melted down all those strips of raw material and put them back inside him. God doesn't waste anything.

Will's business has continued to grow. He is still one of the most spiritually attuned people that I know, and he shares many aspects of Jack's vision for transformative kingdom business. Despite his spiritually disciplined lifestyle, he was unable to see how his family values, noble as they were, led him to make decisions that harmed his business practically and spiritually. Though his intention was to show love to his cousin, his lack of boundaries and clear communication hurt his employees, caused him to struggle with resentment toward his cousin, and robbed his cousin of an opportunity to grow.

It's easy to pick out what was wrong with this scenario, but we all need to humbly recognize that we all have facets of our codebook that lead us to make errors just as obvious. Only through the transformative power of God's grace and that same grace flowing through the connection and insight of healthy relationships can we grow past our unhealthy codebooks and learn to speak and think with the language of heaven.

Jack's story is, in some ways, the most challenging. He's as far from perfect as anyone, but he is a man of character, anointing, and vision. Some part of me feels that a man like that, who builds his business on kingdom principles, should be immune to the ebbs and flows of the economy. If his approach still requires growth, adaptation, risk, and failure, how is it better than any other? I don't know—not from the business perspective, anyway. However, from the spiritual perspective, I've seen the trajectory of Jack's journey differently.

Every person who works for him, every place that he visits, every piece of advice or encouragement he gives, all of it releases that same thriving garden. It released it when he was tentatively starting in a new field of work. It released it when his business was growing and thriving. It releases it just as much today when his business is on the brink of collapse.

When Jack does business, I see the same glory as when my wife runs, the same glory as when a room full of people are lost in worship, the same glory as when a preacher is unlocking the mysteries of the Bible. These are all acts of worship, unique in their expression, but equal in the way they reveal God's glory.

Maybe Jack's businesses will always be vulnerable to the effects of time, treachery, and chance.

Maybe that's just how a world with sin in it works. But something tells me that no matter how many of Jack's businesses fail, that same garden will flow from him and everything he touches. Though the reality of his life will not always match what is happening in the spirit, I believe that his life—and his business—will always find its way back to mirroring the reality of the spirit and unleashing God's glory through business.

CHAPTER 6

MY STORY, PART 2

WHEN I WAS twelve, I learned that the things I saw were the result of a gift. This changed me. I thought I was losing my mind. I thought that the devil had decided to ruin my life. Now I had a gift that I could use to bless people, and I dove into it with my whole heart, soul, and mind.

I practiced seeing in the spirit every day. I wrote down hundreds of notes on the things I saw. I spoke with the prophetic leaders at the church almost every week. I read every book I could find about the prophetic. I went to prophetic training meetings every week. I grew as fast as I possibly could.

I shared about the things that I saw as often as

I felt I was supposed to. Sometimes this went great and people were blessed and encouraged. Sometimes this did not go great and people were confused or scared. But I figured I'd work out those kinks before long. I was just a kid; I had plenty of time to learn. Then something happened that threw a wrench in my accelerating engine.

There was a particular leader whom I was growing closest with. He took a special interest in me, took me under his wing, and helped me find my way with the prophetic. This went great at first. He was very kind and understanding, always willing to help.

The first sign of a problem was subtle. I was at a youth trip in the mountains, and while I was there, I saw a lot of demons around the kids there. I called him to process this, but he sounded instantly annoyed.

"I think you've just been eating too much pizza," he said. "Why would the devil bother with a bunch of kids, anyway?"

I couldn't tell if he was trying to make me feel better or just blowing me off, but something felt strange about the interaction. "Too much pizza" was his sort of code phrase for when someone wasn't discerning something accurately. While I wasn't against the idea of my misinterpreting what I was seeing, saying it so flippantly about something I was seeing with my eyes felt disconcerting.

"Why would the devil bother with a bunch of kids?" was equally confusing. I mean, why wouldn't he? Was he saying young people aren't important? Was he saying the devil only has so many resources?

My main problem was that his responses weren't lining up with how I was coming to understand the language of heaven, though I couldn't have articulated it this way at the time. Something about what he said felt wrong. I didn't want to argue with him, though; he was older, he was more experienced, so he must be right. Still, something about the conversation eroded part of the trust that had been building between us.

After the call left me feeling even more troubled, I found a quiet place and spent time with the Lord. As I did, the demonic things I saw got smaller and smaller. The fear I had been feeling melted away. I realized that I had not been looking at the demonic from the perspective of heaven; I had been seeing it from the perspective of a frightened young boy who was away from his parents. It was one of the first times that I realized how important it is to only ever look at the demonic while seated in heavenly places.

All my interactions with this leader from then on felt off. Maybe it was because our last conversation put me on guard, or maybe it was because something in his life was coming unraveled. I never got to find out. A few months later, he vanished from my life. I found out that he had been asked to leave the church. Some said it was because of a drinking problem, some said it was because of predatory behavior toward a high school student, and some insisted it was the blowback of church politics; I still don't really know.

This shook me more than I realized at first. True, I hadn't felt great about our last few interactions, but he was still one of the main influences in my life around the prophetic and my burgeoning understanding of the gift of seeing in the spirit. Having him suddenly disappear from my life, especially under such confusing circumstances, put cracks in my foundation that I didn't recognize until much later.

Time passed. I became a teenager. I went to school. I kept learning about the prophetic. I continued to see more in the spirit every day, but for whatever reason, I didn't feel effective or helpful with this gift. Sure, people were blessed when I told them what their personal angel looked like or described how angels danced during worship, but just as much of what I shared confused people.

"Why is my angel holding a vase full of oil? Am I supposed to anoint something?"

"You're telling me there are a dozen angels waiting in the rafters, but what should I do? Do I need to pray something?"

"If that guy has three demons hanging on him, does that mean I should kick him out of the building?"

I felt like I understood barely 10 percent of what I saw, and I was seeing more and more every day. I was getting overwhelmed by the layers and layers of things happening in the spirit at every moment. How was I supposed to even take note of everything that happened? How was I supposed to discern what I was supposed to share? How could I do any of that if I barely understood what I was seeing?

Time continued to tick by, and my view of the world grew wider. I learned about history, the news, and life outside the bubble I grew up in. The same penchant for questions I had for the prophetic and the things I saw in the spirit began filling my mind with larger existential concerns.

> If we all have personal angels, if God's presence is with us, and if the Holy Spirit is inside us, then why do bad things happen?
>
> Why do some struggle and starve while others live every day unsatisfied with having more than they need?

Do people have better lives because they
are godlier? It doesn't always seem that
way.

I shared some of these concerns with people
around me, leaders included, but all their answers
either felt like cheap excuses or that they were
evading the point.

If church is made up of God's people, then
why do they bicker, compete, backstab,
and backtalk just as much as the people
they call lost?

If we're supposed to be known for our
love, then why does everyone I tell I'm a
Christian expect so much hate?

Still, everyone's answers to these questions felt like
the kind of wisdom you'd find in a fortune cookie,
a cardboard platitude that evaded reality and was
propped up with ignorance.

Why are there hurricanes that wipe cities
off the map?

Why are there earthquakes that kill
thousands?

Why are children born with bone cancer?

I'm not trying to be crude or callous. I just don't understand.

And then, in the middle of this rising emotional tumult, I read about a mental disorder called schizophrenia: hallucinations, psychosis, and delusions. When I was a kid, the concern for my sanity only had a broad and cartoonish name: crazy. Now I was reading about numerous cases of people who had all kinds of complex delusions. Sure, a lot of the symptoms didn't fit my experience—but I would think that, wouldn't I?

> **How did I know** that I wasn't delusional?
>
> **How did I know** that anything I believed was real?
>
> **How did I know** the Bible was real?
>
> **How did I know** Jesus was real?
>
> **What are the chances** that I just happened to be born into the right religion?

I'll take a quick moment, once again, to step outside the narrative, if only to give us a quick break from the rapid downward spiral of my teenage mind.

Based on the flow of the book so far, you could

probably guess that this crisis of faith gets resolved eventually. Either that or you are quickly thumbing through a file in your head marked "Easy answers to hard questions" and deciding whether "He's deceived" or "It's church hurt" is a better fit. While my crisis of faith no doubt had a lot to do with the painful experience I had with that prophetic mentor, dismissing my pain with "You're only questioning your faith because of a person" is a bit like walking up to someone bleeding on the floor and saying, "You're only dying because you got stabbed."

I don't say this because I need your empathy personally; this season of my life is long past, and you'll see why and how in due course. I say this because I have seen so many Christians respond in a way that inadvertently drives people off the cliff of unbelief rather than away from it.

I get it; it's scary to see someone sliding toward that cliff. Your heart tells you to do something, to say something. However, I find this impulse often drives us to two problems: creating answers to questions that God is not answering and minimizing or ignoring real problems in the church.

The Bible is full of unanswered questions. The Book of Ecclesiastes is full of these questions, Job is a book almost fully dedicated to an unanswered question, many psalms explore the pain and confusion of living with these mysteries, and even Jesus left many parables unexplained and many of the truths He taught about the kingdom unclearly defined.

If it is our goal to eliminate all mystery, then we will inevitably come to conclusions that are incorrect, incomplete, or that actively grind against God's design. These kinds of answers will only drive a person toward the cliff of unbelief faster.

Also, though I love the church with all my heart, we must acknowledge that she is not yet the spotless bride she is called to be. I have loved every church I've been a part of, I have been blessed by every church I have been a part of, and I have been hurt by every church I have been a part of. Some of this was caused by individuals, some of this was caused by unhealthy cultures and systems within a particular church, some of this was caused by broad cultural trends sweeping across the American church, and some of this was caused by historical trends in the global church.

Then what do you do when you see a friend or loved one sliding toward the cliff? You stick close with them, and you love them. If that sounds like an overly simply answer, then you're not hearing me yet. Love is a trying and costly endeavor. Love is sitting in the middle of pain with someone who is hurting. It is fighting the fear that drives you to try to control them and their decisions. Love is coming all the way down to where someone is and staying with them. How do I know this? It's what Jesus did for all of humanity. He came all the way down to humanity's level. He lived a human life. He sat in pain and suffering for us. Love looks like a lot of things. This is one of them.

You can practice on teenage me if you'd like; suppress the impulse to find an answer for me, and just ride this roller coaster for a while. I know it's scary for a lot of you. I'm not encouraging anyone to actively question their beliefs; maybe it *is* better to never have a crisis of faith. Crisis can lead to disaster, this is true, but it can also lead us to what we need. We like to bash on good old doubting Thomas for his unbelief, forgetting that this led to him touching the holes in Jesus' hands and the wound in His side.

With that said, let's get back to teenage me.

I didn't know if I had a mental disorder or was seeing in the spirit.

I didn't know if I believed in God.

I didn't know if I believed in Jesus.

Any Christian I spoke to about this either offered empty answers or was so frightened by my struggle that I quickly learned to stop talking about it.

Feeling lost and alone, I did the only thing that felt like a way forward. I set everything I had ever believed on the table, I stopped talking about the things I saw, and I decided to start exploring what

I believe. I figured that if God was anything close to who I thought He was, He could make Himself known to me.

CHAPTER 7

THE LANGUAGE OF HEAVEN, PART 2

L EARNING A SECOND language is hard work. Anyone who has learned or has attempted to learn a new language knows this. You start by memorizing a few words and some key phrases, but the process is slow. If you sit at a table full of people speaking fluently, you'll understand parts of the conversation. You'll be able to read whether the subject is humorous or serious based on some of the universal aspects of body language and tone. But you may find, if you ask for a translation of the conversation, that the handful of words you understood and your impression of the tone led you wildly astray from the actual subject of the conversation.

This is one of the uphill stages of learning a new language, where frustration and disappointment cause many to give up. I'm not sure where you're at in your journey of discovering the language of heaven, but I hope that taking a moment to dwell on another layer of how this language works will help you make your way up the next stage of this hill.

We already discussed viewing love as one of the key rules of grammar in the language of heaven. This is undoubtedly the most important part of understanding this language and the culture it comes from. But there is another that is almost as important: the relationship between metaphor and literalism.

I am often asked why so many angels appear wearing armor, holding spears, or dressed in robes. Why don't they wear bulletproof vests and sneakers and carry machine guns? This, I think, is best answered by asking a larger question: What are you actually seeing when you see in the spirit?

Not to get too scientific, but what we call seeing is a phenomenon caused by light bouncing off objects and entering our pupils, and our optic nerves interpreting that light into a signal that our brains then interpret into an image.

It is my opinion that what I or anyone else who sees in the spirit is seeing has nothing to do with the physical act of seeing. I mean that I don't think ambient light is bouncing off an angel and into my eyes. I believe that what I am seeing is an open vision, a prophetic picture. Open visions, like most prophetic imagery, are both literal and metaphorical. Understanding in which ways they are literal and which ways they are metaphorical is how we master this piece of grammar in the language of heaven.

It's like the icons on your smartphone. When you swipe your finger just so, one set of icons slides to the side, making room for a new screen of icons. The icons did not literally slide into the void to the left of your phone when you did this. They did not, in fact, move at all, not really. The interactions you have with the icons on your phone are a representation, a metaphor, of the phone's operating software, your applications, and the underlying data by which they all function together.

I want to avoid getting too technical, because this is not a software development book, but the way we use computers and smartphones is a helpful comparison. The raw data and code behind the software we use every day would be completely incomprehensible to most of us. Because of this, clever designers have developed graphical user interfaces, intuitive ways for people to interact with complex computer systems in a way that they can more easily understand.

Are angels literally wearing armor, holding spears,

and dressed in robes? I don't think so, but I do think that the armor they wear, the spears they carry, and the robes they are dressed in are a metaphorical picture of who they are and what they are here to do.

MYSTERY AND METAPHOR

I used to work in the meat department at a store on the north side of Atlanta. I was cleaning up one Friday evening, keeping one eye on the clock as it approached closing time. I had finished all my main tasks, so I decided to take my time cleaning the large windows that looked out on the store floor. All the other workers had already left, leaving me plenty of time to work quietly and think.

As I cleaned the windows, I started looking at all the people walking around the store. I've never met anyone who didn't have a personal angel, and there wasn't a single exception walking in front of the meat department.

I started thinking about the logistics of all this as I watched the waves of Friday night shoppers pick up their New York strips and chuck roasts. Right now there are nearly eight billion people on this planet, with a little more than four being born and a little less than two dying each second. That's a lot of angels for a lot of people! Are there eight billion angels? Did they have to start pulling double duty once we passed a billion?

As I considered this, a man came in front of the window and started looking at the steaks. He was wearing a nice sweater that matched his nice jeans and complemented his nice shoes. He had close-cropped hair, dark skin, and a kindly confident posture; he looked like a nice person.

His angel was about a foot taller than he was with a thin and gently masculine face. He didn't look up at me as I stared at him, standing stoic by his person's side. He wore a pale-blue cloak that looked like it had been made for traveling.

"What happens when their person dies?" I wondered. "Do they just look for someone else? Are they assigned? Can they veto someone they don't like? Is there a raffle?"

The angel with the well-dressed man looked up as if my thoughts had been spoken out loud. As soon as our eyes met, I was pulled into a vision. I knew that I was standing in the meat department, and I could still see my surroundings, but all my attention was pulled toward the vivid images that ran through my head.

I saw a young black woman giving birth, the angel with the blue cloak standing by her side. It was a perfect baby girl, and the angel looked just as excited as the mother. I watched the girl grow up. I saw a Christmas when her mother couldn't afford to buy the dolls the girl wanted but instead gave her some secondhand toys from the thrift store. I watched as her father shouted and drank his way in and out of her life. The angel was always there to hold her when tears poured from her eyes and hide her when her father's anger turned physical.

I saw the angel comfort her when the kids at school made fun of her clothes and teach her when there was no one there to help with her homework. I watched him laugh when she first learned to ride a bike and weep the first time she used drugs to numb the wounds her father gave her.

The angel was with her when she left home in rage, swearing to never come back, and he stayed with her the first time she sold her virtue to keep from starving. Years of brokenness and pain wore away most of the little girl left in her face, but still the angel followed her, caring for the woman the way he cared for the child.

I saw a dark alley drenched in nighttime rain and a man with darkness in his heart taking what dignity she had left by force. The angel stood over her, a sword in each hand, fighting off the encroaching darkness with absolute fury. He struck at shadows with cackling faces as they poured into the alleyway. His blows fell faster than the beat of a rolling drum. He leapt from side to side, throwing himself in the way of any shadow that came near her.

His fight was beautiful, and it was terrible. It was a peak athlete giving everything he had. It was a master dealing in his craft. It was desperation. I've never seen anyone fight so hard for anything. But still the darkness closed in, leaving the woman with bruises on her neck where defiling hands had squeezed out her last breath. The angel fell to his knees, bleeding and bruised; then the image faded.

Next I saw another mother giving birth. This time the angel with the blue cloak smiled down at a baby boy. I watched him grow up with piles of presents at Christmas given by roomfuls of uncles, aunts, and grandparents who all knew how to love. The angel helped push the boy on his first bike alongside the boy's father. I watched his parents provide for the boy's every need. They weren't wealthy, but they weren't wanting.

The angel stood by the boy's side while his father taught him about business and finances. He cheered at graduations, shouted at football games, and laughed at awkward school dances, always accompanied by parents with smiling faces. I watched as the boy grew into the young man who stood in front of me, picking out steaks for dinner.

Then I saw another picture. The young man was driving through the streets of downtown Atlanta on a dark and rainy night. The blue-cloaked angel rode in the passenger seat. As the well-dressed man came to a stoplight, the angel reached out a hand and pressed it against the man's chest. The car came to a slow stop, even though the light was green. With his other hand the angel pointed out the passenger window at a dark alley.

Hesitance written across his face, the man got out of his car and walked down the alley. The angel followed. There the man found a dead prostitute next to a dumpster. The angel in the blue cloak knelt, weeping over the girl, while the same angel also walked by the well-dressed man's side. The kneeling angel stood, made eye contact with himself, and then vanished so that he only remained with the man.

The hesitant expression still hanging on his face, the man leaned over the dead woman and laid his hand over her heart. Immediately the empty lungs filled and the girl arched her back as life came rushing back to her. The man helped her to her feet and then to his car. They drove off in the pouring rain, the angel riding in the back seat.

I wiped the tears from my face and looked at the blue-cloaked angel who stood on the other side of the meat department window.

"Did that already happen?" I thought.

The angel shook his head. No.

I understood his meaning. "Then, will it happen like that?" I asked in my mind. "Will he save her?"

The angel looked down and gave a resigned smile. I saw the answer on his face more clearly than if he had said it out loud: "He could."

———

This story has often reemerged in my memory whenever I find myself trying to understand the logistics of the spirit realm. I was wondering about the technical function of personal angels and the administrative structure by which they operate. The answer I got, if you want to call it that, was a vision so affecting that I can hardly even think about it without being brought to tears. Does this mean that I was asking the wrong kind of question? Not necessarily.

If we look at this story purely as an answer to my specific technical question, we could emerge with a few reasonable clarifications about how the spirit realm works: angels do not seem to relate to time and space the same way that we do, meaning that there does not necessarily need to be eight billion angels to accommodate the population of the earth. Though this answers a technical question, I imagine you would all agree that if this is the only thing we learned from this story, we have missed the point.

I walked away from this story with one overarching truth that still affects the way I think about everything I see in the spirit. All the complexities, intricacies, and details of how the spirit realm functions are designed to serve a singular purpose: revealing God's nature.

Beyond that, this story left me with far more mysteries and questions than it did answers. Why was the angel powerless to save the girl? Was the darkness more powerful than the light? Was she just a victim of another person's evil application of their free will? Was she a victim to the consequences of her own actions? If so, then how is this just when she was born into such a hard life?

I believe that this story is, more than anything else, an invitation to engage in mystery. It is not trying to answer the questions I have about it. It's revealing God's nature. It's not a story about why the angel was unable to stop the darkness. It is a story about how hard he fought to stop it. It's not a story about why bad things happen. It's a story about how heaven responds to the bad things that do happen.

I saw this vision nearly thirteen years ago now, and I still have all the questions I had right after I saw it. However, I also still feel the passion and care the angel showed from the moment the woman was born to the moment she died; I still feel the revelation of a love vaster than my heart can contain. I feel it as if I saw it five minutes ago.

I am reminded of the blind man Jesus and His disciples came upon in John 9. They asked Jesus whose sin had caused him to be born blind, his parents' or his own. Jesus answered by saying that it was neither; it was so that the works of God might be displayed in him.

Does this mean that God made this man blind so

that Jesus could impress everyone with a miracle? I don't think so. I think that Jesus is correcting the disciples' understanding of the language of heaven. They had a preconceived notion about heaven's justice with regard to sin and blindness. Jesus adjusted their perspective, but what He said left a lot of room for mystery.

If we want to get close to God, we need to grow comfortable with mystery. This doesn't mean we stop asking questions; it doesn't mean we just throw anything that doesn't make sense into a big bin labeled "Mystery" and forget about it. It means that we get comfortable with the pain of not knowing, that we learn to continually process the pain of things not working the way we expect, and that we look for what God is saying rather than obsessing over what He is not.

How the Moon Works

In an earlier section I described seeing an angel wearing silver armor who looked like he was in his midfifties. I don't think angels interact with time the way we do, so saying an angel is in his fifties isn't very true from a literal perspective. I believe, however, that it is a true picture of that angel's nature. But what is that picture meant to imply? What does it mean? Well, that is where things can get tricky.

Metaphors are not, by nature, concrete. They measure things that are difficult to measure with numbers. They say the things that are impossible to say.

They describe the reality between all the facts. If that sounds a bit wonky and imprecise, that's because it is. Metaphors are easily misinterpreted, misapplied, and misunderstood. This is why, no matter how much experience or expertise any of us have with the prophetic, seeing in the spirit, or any other gift of the spirit, we must have the humility to accept that we always have the capacity to misunderstand, misapply, or misinterpret the things we hear, sense, and perceive.

Though some of you may be resistant to the idea of metaphor being a keystone of the language of heaven, it is a reality we are going to have to accept. God has consistently shown us that it is part of the way He wishes to present Himself, His kingdom, and His nature to us.

From the visions of the prophets in the Old Testament to the parables of Jesus to the open visions throughout the Book of Revelation, the Bible is absolutely brimming with metaphor. Some of the most horrendous biblical misinterpretations in history stemmed from someone misunderstanding the relationship between the literal and the metaphorical in these passages.

You may not enjoy the potential for imprecision this creates, but it is clearly a fundamental part of God's design for communicating to us. Though I am hesitant to speculate why He would design things this way, I had an experience with one of my kids that gave me a small picture of why this might be.

One night I was driving home with my son in the back seat. He was three years old and getting very adept at using his newfound skill of speaking to ask questions about absolutely everything. It was nearly dark, and it just so happened that when we pulled into our driveway, the trees in our front yard almost perfectly framed the light of the full moon. I watched my son in the rearview mirror as he looked up and saw the moon; his little nose twitched as he formed the question in his growing mind.

"Dad?"

"Yeah, son?"

"How does the moon work?"

Now, I'm not sure if you've noticed this about me yet, but I am a big fan of science. So when my son asks me an open question about the moon, a filing cabinet in my brain shoots open and everything from my third-grade trifold presentation on the moon to a PowerPoint presentation I did in high school comes flying out.

I thought about telling him how the moon affects the tides as well as the earth's orbit around the sun. I thought about telling him about the moon's synchronous rotation with the earth, and how it caused the same side of the moon to always be facing the earth's surface. I thought about telling him how earthquakes on the moon are called moonquakes, how perilous the first moon landing was, and how much lighter he would be if he was standing on its surface.

As I lined up all the sweet moon facts I was about to drop in my son's lap, I looked back at his adorably eager face and realized something. If I threw all my knowledge about the moon at him, he would probably be overwhelmed. He did not have the secondary knowledge and context needed to understand most of what I had to say. In fact, if I just dumped it all on him, he may not ask again next time.

I waited for a moment and considered how to tell him as much information about how the moon works as was possible, based on where he was at, what he could handle. As I went through this brief mental exercise, I had a sudden realization: "This is what God does with us constantly."

The gap between my knowledge and my son's was nothing compared to the gap between my knowledge and God's. God has an understanding and context that is infinitely larger than mine. Maybe some of the questions I ask Him, the mysteries I am baffled by, and the things I perceive as inconsistencies are just like my son asking me how the moon works.

Maybe the places where the Bible uses metaphor are the places where the limits of human capacity would prevent us from being able to even begin to conceptualize the true answer. Maybe the kingdom of heaven is so vast, beautiful, and complex that Jesus was only able to tell us in parables what it is like.

Being comfortable with mystery and willing to

pursue understanding through the limits of metaphor is essential to learning the language of heaven.
We are dealing with a being who is beyond the scope
of our human experience but, thankfully, one who
has invited us to know Him. Just like the oversimplified answer I ended up giving to my son when he
asked how the moon works, God is not being aloof
or vague out of malice or a lack of care. I believe that
He desires for us to know as much of who He is as
possible. I think that metaphor and mystery are key
parts of the language of heaven because learning He
is unknowable is part of learning to know Him. It is
a strange dichotomy but one we must learn to engage
if we want to know God more.

C. S. Lewis, a master at exploring the mystery and
metaphor of God's nature, said it well in his essay
"The Weight of Glory":

> Heaven is, by definition, outside our experi-
> ence, but all intelligible descriptions must be
> of things within our experience. The scriptural
> picture of heaven is therefore just as symbol-
> ical as the picture which our desire, unaided,
> invents for itself; heaven is not really full of
> jewellery any more than it is really the beauty
> of Nature, or a fine piece of music.[1]

Is seeing an angel in silver armor that looks like
a man in his fifties a product of that angel's nature

or my perspective? I think, inevitably, it is rooted in both. To some degree, I think many people see angels with swords and armor because it is what they expect to see. So then how can we trust in the validity and accuracy of any of it? We will get to the heart of this in a later chapter, but for now let me give you a few bumpers to keep you from flying too far off the rails.

First we must respect and honor the authority of Scripture. It's fashionable to call even this into question these days, but I think Lewis says it very well in the statement that immediately follows the one above:

> The difference is that scriptural imagery has authority. It comes to us from writers who were closer to God than we, and it has stood the test of Christian experience down the centuries.[2]

Any image or vision or interpretation that does not align itself with the message and heart of Scripture is wrong. To step away from this is to invite chaos. However, even this we need to approach with a great deal of humility. As we discussed above, the images and metaphors of Scripture have often been misunderstood or misapplied by well-meaning readers and teachers. This is why the second bumper is so important.

All the gifts of the Spirit are designed to function within the context of a community. The only way to protect yourself from your own misinterpretation and misunderstanding of the spirit realm and the Bible is to consistently live in the iron-sharpening-iron dynamic of a healthy community. I know that not every community is healthy, and I know that you may not know where to find one that is. Still, I think that an imperfect community is better than none at all. The lessons we learn when navigating life with an unhealthy community, even when those lessons involve healthy separation from individuals in that community, are essential to our spiritual health.

As Christians we are often taught to be afraid of being deceived. Not to make things worse, but that fear is often just as direct a path toward deception as any other. It makes us rigid, stagnant, and resistant to broader understanding. There is value in being slow to accept new ideas, but remember, our God is infinite, and you do not know all there is to know about Him yet. Resistance to a new idea can be resistance to a deception or resistance to God's nature. Sometimes it's hard to know.

I am not asking you to lower your vigilance. I am asking you to increase it, take ownership of it, and build up some muscles around it. Many of us find our security in our faith by holding fast to the teaching of a few select individuals and rejecting anything that contradicts them. This is not the worst thing in the world. There are a lot of amazing and gifted Bible teachers and prophetic voices out there. However, this puts a lot of power in the hands of an inevitably flawed human being. If instead we take responsibility for studying the Bible ourselves, follow the voices of people whose words point to Jesus, and embed ourselves in a community of others who are doing the same, we are much better equipped to navigate this reality, and we are much more likely to learn the language of heaven well.

CHAPTER 8

A HEALTHY DIET

WHEN I WAS a teenager, my family and I went to the movies almost every week. I have two sisters, and my dad only made it to the movies with us about half the time because of work. This set of circumstances led to me seeing almost every romantic comedy theatrically released between 1998 and 2005. It's not a particularly impressive achievement, but it's one of mine.

One day we went to a matinee showing of one of these movies. I don't remember which one exactly. I think it was the one where a girl and a guy meet unexpectedly, don't like each other much at first, but then suddenly realize that they are in love. It was about two-thirds of the way into the movie, around the time when a misunderstanding or character flaw was making it seem like these two were never going to work it out, that I started looking around the room at my fellow theater attendees.

It was early enough in the day that the theater was mostly empty; there were only two or three clusters of people spread across the room. First my eye landed on a group of four girls a few rows down from where my family and I were sitting. They were all in their midteens and wore matching expressions of heartfelt concern. Three demons hovered in the air in front of them. They had translucent bat wings, beady little black eyes, and long, spindly fingers. The light from the movie screen filtered down to a point in one of the demons' hands, which twisted the light into a fine thread. The next demon was using its nimble fingers to weave the thread into a series of small cloths. The third demon took each cloth and laid it over the girls' faces, one by one.

Each cloth had a small image woven into its surface. A handsome prince riding up on a white horse, a knight in shining armor rescuing a damsel in distress, a young man pining at a maiden's window—each a cartoonish exaggeration of medieval romance.

I looked around the room again. My eye was drawn to a couple in their midfifties on the opposite side of the room from the group of girls.

They were holding hands and smiling warmly

up at the screen. (This was just about the time the onscreen couple was finally overcoming their short-comings and deciding to try again.) The same light fil-tered down from the screen onto the married couple, but no demons surrounded them. Instead, the light landed on their shoulders and arms, and across their embracing hands. Wherever the light touched, little green sprouts emerged on their skin. These grew into multicolored flowers with images on each of the petals. There were images of a wedding, dinner dates, and walks on the beach, all featuring differently aged versions of the couple sitting in the theater.

What's going on here? Is this a good movie or a bad movie? Should I watch it or not? Was that just a bad part of the movie? Well, it's not quite that simple.

For the rest of the movie, I split my attention between the group of girls and the married couple. The spiritual atmosphere around each group remained the same. The demons continued weaving their little cloths, and the couple kept sprouting loving memories.

The demons were weaving the story into unhealthy expectation, trying to establish a destructive perspec-tive of romantic relationships. Is all romance bad? I don't think so. But these demons were trying to rein-force a version of romance that would harm these girls' future.

Strangely, almost the exact opposite was hap-pening with the married couple. The light from the movie was revealing and awakening the romantic parts of their story, reminding them of the beauty of their journey together, and perhaps even raising their romantic expectations in a way that would inspire new life in their marriage.

So, should only married couples over fifty watch romantic movies? No. Remember, we're not memorizing a dictionary; we're learning a language. As I said before, I've seen a lot of romantic comedies, and I've seen them affect people in dozens of different ways. I've seen demons use the content of a movie to hammer a wedge between a husband and wife. I've seen an angel collect the light from a movie into a bowl and pour it over a young woman's head, cultivating healthy romantic hope.

All fiction is fantasy to one degree or another. Most romantic movies are just as fantastical as movies with fairies and trolls, and both of these are just as fanciful as the ones where a man falls through a plate glass window, lands on a car, and then jumps up just in time to shoot the bad guy. Are these fantasies good or bad? Again, I don't think it's quite that simple.

Most of the people who ask me about the spiritual significance of movies seem to be thinking of it the same way you might think of infection or disease. Is this movie infected? Is it going to get something on me? Instead, I think it is more helpful to think of all art and entertainment as food. Sure, food can carry disease, and I've seen some movies and other art pieces that carry disease, but that is not the case as often as you'd think. And like a rotten piece of fish or milk that has gone lumpy, it's really not that hard to discern when something is unfit for your consumption.

Most art and entertainment is more a matter of how and how much you consume it. Some creative expression is rich and healthy like fruit and vegetables. There are plenty of movies, music, and books that I only see good things around. Again, that doesn't mean you can't get hurt by these things. You can still choke on a piece of lettuce, but this has nothing to do with how healthy the lettuce is. I have seen people's wounds cause them to receive a godly message as an attack. I have seen a demon twist a completely innocent song lyric into a harmful message, using a painful piece of someone's history as the vector.

Other art is more akin to, let's say, popcorn. Not the unhealthiest thing in the world, but if it's the only thing you eat, you're probably going to get sick. Watching your favorite show and relaxing can be a great way to rest. I've seen angels ministering peace and restoration to someone as they watch a favorite episode of a comedy series, reread a favorite book, or go for a walk while listening to a favorite album. I've also seen all these things be done with a demon nearby, offering false comfort that leaves the person more tired and anxious by the end.

Some art is like dessert. It's not good for you. Too much can cause several different kinds of problems. But a little can be worth the enjoyment it brings. This is a tricky one. I meet a lot of people who enjoy action movies, crime documentaries, and thrill-a-minute shows with ever-heightening drama. I'm not going to tell you not to consume these things, much as some of you perhaps wish I would. I've seen the same kind of variation in spiritual activity as the stories above. Sometimes I see no negative spiritual effect, sometimes I see a lot of harm being done, and sometimes I see a surprising amount of good.

When I was in school, I lived in an apartment with three roommates. One night the guys were watching a show that I didn't feel great about. The first few minutes had more rough language, violence, and sexual content than I felt comfortable with, so I sat in a corner where I couldn't see the TV, threw on some headphones, and read a book.

I peeked up after a few minutes and saw a demon wandering around the room. It cantered from person to person, swinging its hips in what would be a suggestive way if it weren't being done by something half rotted and sickly. It ran its hands over each person, pulling at little threads that stuck out from their necks, shoulders, and arms. If a thread started coming loose, the demon would pull and pull until the thread hung out completely.

I looked more closely at one of the threads as I walked past my roommate to get a glass of water and saw that it had a little tag at one end, as did each of the threads. On each tag was a single word, and each was different. There were words like *titillate, excite, conquer, win, and fight*. The demon was pulling strings of motivation, using the scenes and ideas in the show as an opportunity to try to manipulate my roommates' drivers.

Some might disagree with me, but I don't think we're drawn to unhealthy media because we're just attracted to darkness or being tempted by sin—at least, I don't think it's as plain as that. I think we are designed to be driven by action, conflict, and sex, and I don't think any of those drivers are evil. They just all have their own appropriate place in life.

We all have a drive to eat. This drive is good. It keeps us from being dead. Unfortunately, I think the drive that was designed to make us seek out rich, tasty fruit and berries gets sabotaged when it encounters the hyperkinetic jolt found in sugary sodas and tasty cakes. Are these things evil? Some of my more health-conscious friends think so, but regardless I think we can all agree that they can be damaging.

Do I think the show my friends were watching was evil? I don't know about that. I know the demon was trying to use it to do evil to them. Just as a hyper-sweet soda can short-circuit our bodies' healthy desire for sugar, I think the demon was trying to use the hyperreal expression of violence, drama, and sex to short-circuit my roommates' healthy drivers in these areas.

All right, so this must mean that this is a bad show and no one should watch it, right? Well, again, it's not quite that simple.

After I sat back down and picked up my book, I looked up at my friends again and realized that the demon was not the only spiritual thing happening in the room. Just as I sat down, a small sparkle shot out of the television and landed on the carpet in the middle of the room. One of my roommates' angels walked up to the place it landed and picked it up. It was a small lump of gold, unrefined, flecked with rock, but unmistakably gold. The angel carried it over to my roommate, squeezed the lump in its hand, and a thin stream of pure liquid gold ran through its fingers and into my roommate's chest. This same process happened three more times in just the few minutes I watched for it.

Art belongs to God. He created it. He designed it. Does this mean that all art is godly? No. But it does mean that the process, the form, the fundamental nature of art is of Him. Though the show my roommates were watching was full of content that was not beneficial, and though a demon was using aspects of the show as an opportunity to manipulate them, that does not mean there was nothing good in it. There was no explicitly godly message in the show, but I am sure it contained artful depictions of human nature, real emotion, and real experiences, and that those depictions were birthed from the soul of a person who was made in the image of God.

Why is this important? Well, I think that many Christians, in an attempt to protect themselves and others from the real harm that imperfect art can cause, throw the proverbial baby out with the bathwater. This can cause us to become stagnant, missing out on pieces of God's nature that we might not encounter elsewhere, and it can cause us to miss out on an opportunity to pick up that piece of gold and show someone where it came from.

So where does this leave us? Watch whatever you want; everything has gold in it? Definitely not. It may be just a metaphor, but I believe it is a helpful one: think of all the art and entertainment you consume as food. I can't tell you when you've had too much cake. But I know that you can. I know that we are all capable of fooling ourselves in this area; I have seen the bottom of enough bags of chips and cookies to be honest with myself about that. Maybe the people who don't eat any sugar, throw their TV out the window, and eat nothing but salads and quinoa are right. For now, I'll just say be a thoughtful eater. Don't try to eat chicken wings the way you eat popcorn. Don't eat a lobster the way you eat an apple. You've got to eat the meat and spit out the bones.

All art is deeply spiritual. It all influences you. If you don't think so, then you've either gone numb in that area or the influence has already been integrated into your way of thinking. Either way, it's a place worth paying attention to, especially since, in the age we are in, art and entertainment can fly at you at a million miles an hour.

CHAPTER 9

YOUR GARDEN

I WANT TO TELL you about my friend Joey. Joey is a wonderful guy. He's smart and funny, he's handsome and charming, and he loves Jesus with his whole heart. Despite all this, Joey's life is always in shambles.

He was divorced when I met him and has been in a custody battle with his ex-wife for as long as I've known him. He always has a good idea for a business, and they all start out with initial success, but after a while they fizzle and fail. He makes friends fast. It has always been easy for him to insert himself in a group of friends, but after a year or two, none of those people are connected to him anymore. Joey is always optimistic; he always puts his faith in the

Lord to see him through, but for some reason the Lord always has to see him through a lot.

Why do these things keep happening? What is Joey doing wrong? Is the devil messing with him? Is there secret sin in his life? Let's walk this through slowly. We're learning a language, and there is a lot of helpful grammar in Joey's life. Of course all his circumstances are unique to him, but I have met hundreds of people stuck in similar cycles. If you can catch some of the key pieces of language here, you will be able to help people out of these cycles, and you might be able to get out of a few of your own.

First of all, Joey walks with a limp—not physically, but in the spirit.

Everyone has wounds: the bumps, bruises, and cuts of everyday life, as well as the breaks, gashes, and scars of trauma. No two of us have the same story, but this kind of pain and hurt is part of all our stories. Sometimes the results of this harm are long lasting. It may affect the way we act, think, see, or walk through our daily lives. For Joey, this looks like a limp.

One time Joey was out of work and staying with a friend. The friend had an extra room; he even had space for the kids when Joey had them on the weekends. Joey looked for a job all the time, but nothing was a good fit, nothing made quite enough money, nothing was heading in the direction his life was heading, and nothing came to fruition.

I was over visiting one day during this time. Joey was going on and on about how hard the job market was, how difficult it was to find something that still left time to be with his kids, how he knew that God was going to work it out, and how grateful he was about how God was taking care of him through this hard time.

The person he was staying with at the time was in the room as well. As Joey spoke, every move and gesture sent dirt and dust in the direction of his friend. Particles of dirt hit him in the face and eyes, causing him to flinch a few times. When Joey talked about "how God was taking such good care of him," I saw a strip of flesh peel off the side of Joey's friend's face. Joey was a kind person, but he had a hard time seeing the difference between being provided for by God, depending on the kindness of others, and taking advantage of someone's generosity. This was hurting his friend. Within a few months, the friend asked him to leave.

Not long after that, Joey came to me super excited. He had a great idea for a new business, and several people already wanted to invest. He wanted me to look in the spirit and see if this was God's will for his life.

I told him that I wasn't sure if I'd be able to tell if that was the case, but I'd be happy to look. I saw an angel holding a silver tray. On it was everything Joey needed for his business: piles of money for the initial investment, plans and procedures to structure the business, cards with the names of all the people he needed to connect with, and a stack of small jars that were filled with glowing golden oil. Spiritually speaking it looked like everything had been arranged; even the anointing for each stage of the process was already available.

Joey was thrilled. He gave me a big hug, thanked me, and turned to leave. As he turned, he limped a bit, knocking into the angel and sending a few of the jars of oil smashing to the ground.

A few months passed by. Joey got all the equipment he needed for his startup business, he started a grassroots marketing campaign, and lots of his friends pitched in to help. Every time I saw him, I saw the angel with the tray of supplies, and every time the supplies were a little more jumbled up and a few more jars of anointing were missing. The business had a great launch, saw initial success, and then faltered. One by one the people who partnered with him stepped away from the project, the money thinned out, and the business ended up being little more than a pile of gear in his garage. The last time I saw the angel with him, all that was left on the silver plate was a single cracked jar of anointing.

Why did his business fail, especially when it was being supplied by heaven? Was it flaws in Joey's character? Was it demonic attack? Was it because of a lack of strong business sense? Did he do something to sabotage the favor on his life? I don't think any one of these is the main reason Joey's business failed, but unfortunately I'd have to say that the answer to all these questions is yes.

Every one of us has a spiritual ecosystem around us, our own personal garden. Everything you think, believe, and do feeds this garden. The way your garden starts out is not always fair. Everyone experiences some level of shame, pain, and abuse, but not all of us experience it to the same degree. These may happen in parts of our early childhood, teen years, or young adulthood, or be consistent throughout our entire lives. Some of these are the consequences of our own choices, but just as many are inflicted upon us without any wrongdoing on our part. Either way, these experiences shape the landscape of our gardens, creating deep ruts and stagnant ponds. They put poison into our soil, choking the good fruit we're trying to grow.

When I looked at Joey's garden, I could see that it was sick. There was a ton of good around him. He loved the Lord. Glowing light swirled around him in beautiful patterns every time I looked at him, a manifestation of Joey's heart for worship and value for the presence of God. He prayed for others with passion and authority. Fresh, clean water from heaven poured down over anyone he laid his hands on. The angel with the silver tray was not the first or the last I saw of its kind around Joey. Heavenly ideas were attracted to him. They came with the anointing and tools needed to come to fruition. Joey's garden attracted good things, but it was also filled with poison.

One day someone came to me to talk about Joey. They wanted to confront him about how his lack of follow-through in certain areas affected the people who had invested in helping him. The person was frustrated and hurt but genuinely wanted to bring healing to their relationship with Joey. I encouraged them to speak with him while remaining as loving as possible through the process, affirming that their goal was to heal the relationship. I saw them arguing in the church parking lot the following Sunday.

It just so happened that my car was parked near where they were standing. I took a wide route, doing my best to give them space.

My approach brought me from behind Joey, who was waving his arms wildly as he spoke, clearly exasperated. A tall demon, covered all over in long fur, stood behind the person confronting Joey with its arms stretched out high and wide, like a bear. Every few seconds the demon produced basketball-sized globs of tar from the palms of its hands. He threw these down, coating Joey in thick, black gunk.

Naturally this made me feel defensive for Joey. I worried that the person confronting him had let their pain get the better of them. But then I walked a bit closer. I curved around the arguing friends in a wide arc, so that I now viewed them from the side, and from this angle the whole scene looked completely different.

I realized that the demon was not standing behind the person confronting Joey; that had been an optical illusion. From the side I could see that the demon was paper thin and standing between the two of them.

An angel stood behind the person confronting Joey. It was using a shovel to dig up the ground around the person. In the soil was a mixture of dirt, rocks, jewels, and gold. It tossed this mixture toward Joey, but the furry demon caught it each time. The clump of treasure and dirt filtered through the demon, was coated in the thick black tar, and fell onto Joey.

I curved behind the person confronting Joey, finally reaching my car. As I got in, I saw from this perspective that it looked like the demon was standing behind Joey, the angel was shoveling pure gold, and the demon was catching it and throwing it on the ground on either side of Joey.

Who was wrong? Who was making the mistake? Who caused the miscommunication? We could blame the demon, but demons can only work with what's already there. We could blame the person confronting Joey for overestimating the value of their feedback and advice. We could blame Joey for not being able to see the value of the feedback he was being given.

If we want to learn the language of heaven, then another important piece of grammar is understanding that all life exists in an ecosystem, a space where life affects life, for good and for bad. This is also true of the spirit realm.

Joey has always been full of faith. He is confident of God as his provider, and God always provided for him. I saw this in the spirit all the time. What Joey failed to do was learn how to steward that provision.

The spirit realm is like an ecosystem. Joey's ecosystem, his garden, was full of faith and dependence on God, but it lacked personal responsibility. I have seen other gardens where this is the opposite. Personal responsibility is thriving; they get a lot of things done and are extremely dependable. However, this overbalanced self-reliance leaves no room for the part that only God could do, making their garden, their spiritual life, a shadow of what it could be.

This is complex, and we need to see it as such or we will miss the point. It's not as simple as adding a dash of faith, two cups of personal responsibility, and then you're done. Your early childhood experiences affect how you see faith, personal responsibility, and all the hundreds of other factors that affect your garden. These are just a few of the stories from Joey's life. I have dozens more; stories that are good, stories that are bad, and stories that I'm still not sure how to categorize. And Joey is just one person. Every person has this much going on and more.

It's easy to get overwhelmed by this—I certainly do—but I think this is because we think we need to solve the problem. We think we should have a pristine garden, perfectly balanced, no insects or pests, and massive fruit of every kind. Maybe this is the goal, but I don't think we get there by letting perfectionism beat us over the head with an unrealistic standard. We get there by learning to cultivate our garden. We check the fruit each season to see what's thriving and what's dying on the vine.

I think this is why the Bible calls it the fruit of the Spirit. Love, joy, peace, patience, kindness, goodness, faithfulness, gentleness, self-control—these are not gifts; they are fruit that is meant to grow in your garden. If any of these are not regularly produced by your garden, then you might need to make an adjustment.

Joey is an interesting case. I have seen people with much messier lives and harder backgrounds than his tend their gardens until they are so lush and healthy that you would think they had never struggled a day in their lives. If you pressed me to pick the top reason why Joey and people like him stay stuck in repetitive cycles of destruction, it would be this: they are usually not very influenceable.

Joey was and is a wonderful man, and I love him

still, but he did not know how to receive feedback. It scared him. It always felt like an attack. I'm not saying I or anyone else ever gave him perfect feedback. The way other people's wounds and deficits clashed with Joey's wounds and deficits is part of the tragedy of his story. It was never all his fault, but it's never all anyone's fault.

Joey came to me one day, desperate. He had lost custody of his kids. I encouraged him, I prayed with him, and then I did something I was very scared to do: I told him about his limp. I talked about the way his wounds affected his life and how they caused these misunderstandings and conflict with the people in his life; I talked about how this invited destruction into his life. I said it as gently and kindly as I knew how. I said it because I believed in him and wanted his life to be whole. I know I didn't say it perfectly, and I know I wasn't seeing his situation perfectly, but I tried to share it for his benefit. But I knew the whole time I spoke that it wasn't working.

With each sentence I saw lines appear across his face. These split open into cuts, trickling blood down his cheeks. I could see, in the physical, his expression tightening. This was not going well.

When I finished, he paused for a moment and then started yelling at me. The wounds on his face burst open like a hundred crisscrossed mouths, spitting blood at me. He didn't speak to me for a year after that.

I could blame Joey for not being able to take the feedback. I could blame myself for the places I didn't give it well enough. I could blame the family he was born into, probably the place he got those cuts that burst open. All this blame would be fair, but none of it would help. I don't know what Joey needs to be able to become influenceable by the friends who love him; by the spiritual mothers and fathers who care for him; and by God, who is providing him with many things, including the grace to grow. I hope that he finds it.

The saddest part of this story is what was standing behind Joey the whole time we spoke. It was an angel dressed in golden armor, holding a sword in one hand and a book with the word *Justice* on the cover. I knew it was heaven's complete provision for the situation Joey was facing—restoration for his relationship with his kids and protection from any demonic influence that would try to get him to believe lies or reinforce the lessons his wounds taught him. It was all there. But when he walked away from our conversation, Joey limped and bumped into the angel, knocking a few pages from the book. I prayed that this would be the last piece of God's provision for his situation that ended up lost on the floor.

The spirit realm is not a separate place. It is part of the grand ecosystem we call creation. Everything affects it. It affects everything. I don't want this to overwhelm you or cause you to grow overly introspective, but I do hope it motivates you to tend your garden. Maybe that looks like investing in the skills and talents of a coach or counselor. Maybe it looks like deepening the intimate connection with your friends and community. Maybe it looks like wholehearted pursuit of the language of heaven through meditation on Scripture, prayer, and the pursuit of God's presence. I think all these things are needed for a garden that is overflowing with the fruit of the Spirit.

CHAPTER 10

PLANS AND PURPOSES

I WAS IN THE middle of a Sunday night service at Bethel Church in Redding, California, when I suddenly had to leave. It was as urgent as the need for a bathroom and as subtle as a whisper in a windstorm, but I knew I had to go. Whether you're in a movie theater, airplane seat, or the middle of a church auditorium, there's no polite way to scoot past a full row of people. I did my best to avoid making any more eye contact than necessary as I knocked knees with every person blocking my way to the aisle, wishing that the urge to step outside had come before everyone had been comfortably seated.

This urge was a relatively new phenomenon. I

usually saw in the spirit, for lack of a better term, casually. I'd either be actively practicing seeing in the spirit or suddenly find myself curious about what was happening, and then I'd just look. There was always something happening. I didn't always understand it, of course, but there was always something there. I looked whenever I had the mind to—that was it. But lately, things had started to change.

It started out as a gentle tug, like a child pulling at the edge of your shirt. It wasn't dramatic. It could easily be ignored. But it was persistent. It was like the Holy Spirit saying, "Hey, I want to show you something."

I had learned to follow this tug, even when it involved being mildly rude to an entire row of churchgoers.

I walked outside and was surprised at how cold it had gotten. I had left my sweatshirt at home, and I didn't have an immediate sense of where the tug wanted me to go. Thinking that my car would at least block out the wind, I made my way up the small hill toward the gravel parking lot, arms crossed against the cold and eyes on my feet. I was halfway up the hill when I realized I wouldn't be making it to my car.

His light shone on the ground in front of me, but I felt his warmth before I saw the light. Hesitant, I lifted my gaze to see a pair of burning feet, flaming legs, and a blazing torso. To say he was engulfed in flames would be an understatement. The fire raged around him so thickly and violently that I couldn't tell if there was an angel somewhere in there or if this was a being made entirely of roaring flame.

This was imposing enough, but it was not the fire that gave me pause. Instead, it was the immense sense of power and prestige that emanated from something inside the flames.

I've been seeing angels my whole life, so it always seemed strange to me when I heard and read about stories where people cowered at the sight of an angel and the angel had to say, "Be ye not afraid." Angels weren't scary. Beautiful, yes. Mighty, sure. But not scary. This angel, however, made me understand why someone might feel afraid.

It was not that he himself was intimidating, or the flames that surrounded him; it was what the flames represented. I probably couldn't have articulated this in the moment, but I could feel that this angel had been in the presence of God in a way that I had not yet—perhaps in a way that I could not yet. He had been close to the Source of all glory, all power, and all knowledge, and the heat his body retained from that proximity caused the air around him to burst into flames. That's the kind of thing worth cowering over.

"Hello," I said, unable to think of a more regal greeting.

Like I've said before, when I hear angels speak, it isn't with English words. Ideas, whole and complete, land in my brain. I can more or less translate these into an English sentence, but in my mind it is an understanding.

"Hello," the angel replied. A more dramatic reply was unnecessary, given his fiery appearance.

"Something I can help you with?" I asked.

At this, the angel pulled a scroll from somewhere behind his back. It was in an ornate case that changed color the way a scarf waves in the wind. He pulled it open, revealing a dark, almost black, blue page with hundreds and thousands of intersecting lines, dots, and circles. In my memory it seems chaotic, but in the moment it was clear that every line was exactly in the place it was meant to be.

"What is it?" I asked.

"It is God's plan as it relates to you."

Then I noticed that all the lines and dots were slowly moving, orbiting, and growing. Dots blinked in and out of existence as connections were made and lost between people. Lines twisted and crossed as every possible choice that every person on the scroll could make interacted with every possible response to every possible choice. My eyes stretched open wide. The more I stared, the more I understood.

The complexity unfolding before me began to press against the borders of my mind. It was too much to comprehend, but I was still trying.

Frightened that I might burst a vital synapse, I shook my eyes free from the scroll and turned back to the angel. It was much easier to see him now, not the flames but the figure beneath, as if my eyes had grown more accustomed to his appearance.

He wore golden armor with molded murals that covered every exposed surface. They clearly told a story, though the plot and characters were unclear to me. Perhaps this was because my brain was still sore from trying to understand what I saw on the scroll. Every inch of him glistened. I want to say that his armor was inlaid with jewels and gems, but this looked nothing like it would on a necklace or engagement ring. Those kinds of jewels are held in place by fixtures and fastenings, but these were part of the gold, like leaves are a part of a tree. Nothing held them together. They were a part of each other.

I spent a lot of time admiring his armor, partially because it was so fascinating, but mostly because I was terrified to look this truly otherworldly being in the eye. Even though I could see him more clearly, the radiant heat that came off him had not lessened at all. It made me feel embarrassed, unclean. That's not quite right, though it's the closest thing to how it felt. There was no shame like the word *unclean* implies. It was as though my body itself was trying to comprehend the difference between myself and the presence surrounding the angel.

This feeling only magnified when I looked into his eyes. This angel had seen God as I had never seen Him. I met God before I could pronounce words like *omnipresent, omnipotent, eternal,* and *holy.* I had only ever known Him as the loving Father, faithful Friend, and patient Teacher.

I saw all these things in the burning angel's eyes and more. I saw a God of mercy and a God of might. I saw the God who conceived ideas like time, gravity, power, and glory. I saw the God who caused Moses' face to shine so brightly that it had to be hidden.

Looking in his eyes was too overwhelming, so I directed my next comment to his feet. "The plans on that scroll look complicated."

This made him laugh. He grabbed both sides of the scroll and turned it horizontally and on its side, as if it were on a table between us. The lines and markings on the page sank down into several layers below the surface of the paper, causing every dot and connection to twist and pulse in three dimensions.

My still-feeble brain struggled to grasp what this meant and how this affected the bits and pieces that

I'd understood when the scroll was in two dimensions. Like an old bicycle desperately trying to snap into gear, my mind did its best, but the chain fell off. It all just looked like a tangled mess of intersecting lines and dots.

I spoke with the angel for what seemed like a long time, though in truth it could have just as easily been ten minutes as four hours. We talked about what kinds of things were coming up in my life and the lives of my closest friends. I met with him twice after that, each meeting instigated by a whispered invitation while I was doing something else.

I thought about this encounter often in the years that followed, and I thought about the scroll. It really did feel like I had started to understand it when it was displayed in a flat two-dimensional image. The angel said that it was God's plan as it related to my life. I don't think I could have used it to predict my future or anything, but I could see, or at least sense, the order behind it.

The dots represented people, moving in and out of one another's lives. The lines represented their trajectory, the places their choices took them, and the ways their lives intersected with mine. The lines were all moving and adjusting; some points remained stable, while others moved erratically. This represented each person's free will and the ways God's plan flexed and bent to accommodate people's choices while remaining true to its purpose.

I didn't understand what I saw clearly enough to weigh in on the age-old debate of predestination and free will; however, I did get the sense that God's plans and purposes could more than handle the fact that He gave us a will. Does that mean we have totally free choices in our lives? Does that mean He gives us choices but arranges circumstances that direct us down a preordained path? I don't know. It's like how the moon works.

Years later I was thinking about the scroll yet again, and I suddenly felt the freedom to ask what it meant when the angel had set it down flat and the image had morphed into three dimensions. So I did. And I got a rare direct answer.

"When the scroll was in two dimensions, you saw people's paths and how their choices affected their direction. When the angel laid it down, you saw their inner world; the way emotions, thoughts, and all the internal struggle that comes with them led to their external choices."

I sat and thought about this for a while. It still didn't really tell me much about the difference between predestination and free will, or whether God sets a singular perfect path for our lives or partners with our godly choices. Instead, it reinforced that however His plans and purposes work, He has considered their outworking more deeply, more intricately, and more intimately than I could possibly imagine.

CHAPTER 11

MY STORY, PART 3

WHEN WE LEFT my story last, I was a lost and lonely teenager, struggling with my faith, uncertain whether I had a gift of the Spirit or was a high-functioning schizophrenic.

A few years passed by without much change. I read books about atheism, Buddhism, Gnosticism, humanism, and even theism. Many of the books I read were asking the same questions I was, but they all had answers just as empty as the spiritual clichés I got from my Christian friends. Some of them were better written, some of them were more honest about their uncertainty, some of them were more logical, some of them were more emotionally intuitive, but none of them rang true.

I wasn't sure what I was looking for, to be honest, but Christianity rang the truest. That could be because it *was* true or because I was raised to believe it. My searching also led me to read about the history of Christianity and all the ways it had changed and morphed in the two thousand years since Jesus. Even if Christianity was the "right" religion, whatever that means, how did I know that the version I grew up practicing was right?

This all may sound like it involved me running away from home, starting a drug habit, or otherwise going full prodigal son. But it didn't. I prefer to think about things slowly and had no intention of making any choice with long-term effects until I decided which direction I wanted to go.

I went to church with my family, I continued seeing in the spirit, I kept going to youth group, and I continued following all the external tenets of Christianity. Apart from my initial questions, I didn't let anyone in on what I was going through. I don't recommend this, but it's what I did. This was an inside journey for me. And like most inside journeys, there was no one thing that made me decide on a direction, but a thousand small ones. There was, however, a tipping point, a part of the journey where I stopped going deeper into the valley of the shadow of death and started walking out.

My church hosted a youth mission trip each year. This particular year, we were sent to Europe. We did some street ministry in Paris and served another youth ministry in Southampton in England. Our youth pastor always liked to put something more fun or relaxing at the end of our trips, and for this one he had arranged for us to go to a large youth concert and conference near London.

There were more than three thousand youth attending the event, which was being held in a massive cattle auction house with double-decker stadium seating. There were so many kids that there wasn't enough space in all the local hotels to accommodate everyone, so the conference organizers had arranged for tents to be available to rent in the fields around the event center.

There was a mixture of worship music and early-2000s techno that would probably be super embarrassing if I heard it now but seemed really cool at the time. There were different preachers and workshops, and fun stuff like DJ classes and dance contests.

Fast-forward to the last night of the conference. We were going to be flying out the next morning, and most of us were tired from the long trip, so we were taking it easy and sitting in the back corner on the upper deck of the arena.

I listened to the preacher for the first few minutes. Years of instincts honed over hundreds of church meetings informed me that he was going to be ending the night with an altar call, inviting people up to the front to receive Christ. Feeling that I was fine to miss that, I leaned back in my chair, put my feet on the empty seat in front of me, and tried to take a nap. I don't know why I looked back down—I had heard a thousand different salvation messages—but for some reason I looked down at the stage again.

It was then that I saw Jesus.

He was pacing back and forth at the front of the room, in the margin between the stage and the chairs. He didn't look like the stereotypical bearded and robed Jesus that I had seen in so many Sunday school coloring books. Apart from the faint glow that engulfed His head, He would not have been out of place in line at the supermarket. But I knew it was Jesus the moment I saw Him.

He continued to pace back and forth, a look of calm concentration on His face. I quickly noticed that every time He turned, His gaze remained fixed at a spot somewhere at the back of the room. I followed His line of sight a hundred or so yards to the back where a girl, maybe a bit older than me, sat with her head slumped against the divider that separated the first row of stadium seats and the main floor.

"He sees no one but her," said a voice somewhere in my head.

The room began to fade as I watched Jesus pace. It wasn't that I couldn't see the room or hear the preacher; it was as if all my senses were so drawn to

Him and what He was doing that anything else faded into the background. So it was distantly that I heard the preacher begin to ask people to come forward if they wanted to be saved.

My eyes snapped back to the girl, and I watched as she lifted her head from the divider and glanced up at the front of the room. I saw Him move, but it took Him no time to get there. Jesus was pacing at the front, and then He stood directly in front of her.

The room was all but gone, the kind words of the passionate preacher far away and muffled. I couldn't feel the ground beneath my feet. I couldn't smell the air around me. Every part of my consciousness was utterly captivated by the scene below.

The girl lifted her head just enough to look Jesus in the eye. Immediately chains appeared around her neck, then her shoulders, and then her waist until she was completely covered, neck to knees. The chains extended from her in four long strings, a demon pulling at the end of each. The demons dragged at the chains, causing her to slump back down. She nestled her face into the crook of her arm as it rested on the divider, breaking eye contact with Jesus. But it didn't matter.

Jesus leaned forward and kissed her on the forehead. As soon as He did this, every link in the chain split in half, starting at her neck and running all down her body like a string of firecrackers. The demons flew back from the loss of tension as the world flashed away in blinding white light.

My vision slowly returned, but the room did not. I couldn't see the preacher, I couldn't see the stage, and I couldn't see the other attendees. I looked down and couldn't even see myself. All I could see was Jesus and the girl.

A lifetime of satisfaction was written on Jesus' face as He stood with His arms open wide. The girl stood wearing white robes, facing Him. It may be something of a Christian cliché, but the robes were whiter than white—the whitest thing I have ever seen, before or since. Jesus beckoned, and the girl lunged forward, sinking her face into His chest and wrapping her arms around Him. I felt embarrassed, like I'd walked in on a private moment, and was just thinking of how to get out of this when I felt a weight from above me.

I looked up and saw a giant hand coming down from the endless pale sky. Each finger was thick as a baseball bat. The index finger extended and touched me on the forehead. As if I'd been dropped into a pool of ice water, I snapped back into reality with such force that I fell backward into my chair. I sat there a moment, feeling shell-shocked, and then leaned forward just in time to see the girl from the back running up the aisle to accept Jesus (even though she already had).

This was a beautiful and powerful vision, one that

is burned into my memory as vividly today as it was the day it happened. But what changed me, what redirected my internal journey and set me on the path I'm on today, is what happened right afterward.

The rest of the meeting swept by in a misty blur. I didn't know it was over until people began pushing past me on their way to the exit. I got up to leave without really thinking about what I was doing. Now, I'm pretty good at getting lost in my own neighborhood in broad daylight, so I was not entirely convinced that I was going to be able to find my way back to the tents where my youth group was staying. I quickly scanned the crowd and found one of the girls from my group. I fixed my eyes on her and trudged through the crowd, hoping she knew where she was going.

I knew this girl, but we weren't best friends or anything. I'd had a dozen brief conversations with her at our church back in California. But as I walked through the crowd, focusing on her, I saw everything there was to know about her life.

I saw every moment of joy, every moment of peace, every moment of fear, and every moment of pain. With each moment I felt every emotion as if I were a brother or a dear friend. I could not look away. I saw every choice she had made, good or bad, and the process that led to each decision. I saw every sin, every lie, and every mistake. I saw secret hopes, hidden dreams, and private prayers. I saw every moment of her future and then every possible future based on every decision she would or wouldn't make. I saw the full measure of her potential and how far she would make it within that potential. Emotions flooded faster than I could comprehend them. Triumph, loneliness, laughter, shame, hope, fear, warmth, sorrow, and elation all swirled and congealed into one impossibly profound whole—love.

Love is a word that has been beaten into many molds, but this was a love that was perfect and complete, the sum of every moment of a life viewed with adoring eyes. It was bigger than anything I'd ever perceived and simpler than anything I'd ever experienced. I suddenly understood why Jesus chose to die on the cross, and in that moment, I would have done the same.

The feeling only grew. It swelled in my mind and overflowed out of my heart; all of me was too small to contain it. It was almost painful. Overwhelmed, I tore my vision from the girl and looked away.

Then my gaze snapped like a magnet onto one of the guys from my youth group. Again, an entire lifetime poured in through my eyes. Again, a love I couldn't explain or contain filled my chest until I yanked myself free to keep from bursting. Then my eyes caught one of the other random conference attendees. I'd never met him, but I knew everything that could be known about him.

Unfortunately, as I mentioned earlier, I was in a

very large crowd. I soon found myself trapped as I bounced from person to person, fighting to keep my brain from erupting. I describe it as a feeling, but this was no idle affection. This love did not require anything of the person, but it demanded to be expressed. I wanted to prophesy over each of them. I wanted to sing to them, to kiss them, to hug them, to pray for them, to grab each of them by the face and scream, "You are loved!" until my lungs burst. But anything I thought to do to express this love was so painfully and woefully inadequate compared to it that I felt paralyzed. Nothing was enough.

Finally, I got a bright idea and stared down at my own feet. This worked for a second, then someone's foot kicked out in front of me, and I kid you not, I saw everything there was to know about their life. I saw every moment of joy, every moment of pain. I saw the fullness of their potential. I saw how far they were going to make it along that line of potential. And I fell completely and totally in love with this person, without ever seeing their face.

Eventually the crowd thinned enough that I was able to find my way back to my tent and immediately fall face-first down into my pillow. Thankfully, when I woke up the next morning, it was gone, because I do not know how I would have been able to function if it were not.

I share this story often. It is without a doubt my

favorite, not just because of the story itself, but because of what it meant for me at that time in my life. This moment did not immediately restore my belief in God, and it did not solidify my belief in my own gifting—but I think it gave me something even better.

I could have, once my overwhelmed senses calmed, picked this vision apart. It wouldn't have been hard at all. I already had a lifetime of Christian belief knocking around in my head. It only made sense that a hallucination would follow the tracks that were already laid in my mind. Throw in a little sleep deprivation and the hype from the conference, and you have a solid recipe for a fake experience.

What surprised me, after my emotions did cool down, was that even though it was easy to see how I could pick apart every piece of the experience, I simply didn't want to. The rational part of my brain wanted to be sure I wasn't tricking myself. The emotional part of my brain still had a thousand unresolved questions and concerns. Despite this, all parts of my brain, every inch of my heart was still enthralled by the love that had flowed through me that day.

I still didn't know how I felt about the church. I still didn't know how I felt about modern Christianity. But I knew that I would gladly do anything that served a love like that.

Piece by piece, day by day, that love led me to picking back up almost everything I had grown up believing. I saw each of these elements in a new light, with a new fire at the center of each, a fire of eternal love. I am now happy to call myself a Christian and happy to be a leader in a church. Do I still have problems with the way parts of the church and Christianity operate today? Yup. But I am willing to walk together with my fellow Christian brothers and sisters, growing into a church worthy to be called the bride of Christ.

Where does that leave my belief about seeing in the spirit? Well, that's interesting. I don't believe in what I see. I believe in Jesus. If what I see points to Him, then I believe it. If it doesn't, I wait, I watch, and I listen until it does. So far, it always has. Do I have a hallucinatory mental disorder? Maybe. Do I think so? No. The fact is that I don't really care, though that may be strange for some of you to hear. I don't need what I see to be part of a special gift. I don't need to be a special person. Everything that I need to be is found in that love I felt in that field in England—a love I still feel today, anytime I take a moment to reach for it; a love that has been burning since before the foundations of the earth; a love that will be here long after the earth is gone; a love that is pointed at me; a love that is pointed at you, now and forever. That's my story.

CHAPTER 12

THE LANGUAGE OF HEAVEN, PART 3

L ET'S TAKE A moment to relook at the story from the previous chapter. We can test our spiritual vocabulary and see how our heavenly grammar is holding up.

The vision started with Jesus pacing at the front, keeping His eyes fixed on her with every step. I heard a voice say, "He sees no one but her."

Is this true? Did Jesus literally only see her? I don't think so. Nearly a hundred kids ran up to the front at the end of the service. Did Jesus not see any of them?

I do not believe the voice I heard was saying something literal, but I believe it was saying something true. Jesus saw everyone in that room, but saying this tends to make His love feel broad and impersonal. I think this is because we too easily apply human limits on God. We would need to shift our focus from the crowd, to an individual, and then to another individual. It would take you or me hours to see everyone individually in a room like that, but God sees the crowd and each individual all at the same time.

Like learning how the moon works, it's easier for my limited mind to comprehend the key message of this vision—"God's love for the one"—if I see Jesus focusing on one person all the way at the back of the room. It communicates this point more clearly.

Could I have seen a similar but different version of Jesus, pacing back and forth, looking at each of the hundred people who came up at the end? Could I have seen a picture of Jesus engaging with all hundred at once? Probably. It's just not what I saw that day.

The preacher invited people to come to the front to receive Jesus. The girl lifted her head. He rushed to her. Chains appeared all around her. She slumped back down. He kissed her on the forehead.

When I think back to this, it all appears with the rhythm and precision of a dance, like it had all been planned ahead of time. That's not to say it seemed inauthentic or staged. The moves of a dance are predetermined, but the dancers are still dancing. Even if they danced the same dance a thousand times, each would not be quite the same.

She lifted her head, the smallest gesture of invitation. Jesus immediately closed the gap between Him and her, an echo of the distance He traveled by setting aside His divinity to cross the gap for all mankind. The chains appeared all around her. They were piled upon one another, thick and heavy. Four demons held her back. She slumped her head down. Even her smallest effort wasn't enough. She was so impossibly bound.

Then Jesus leaned down and kissed her forehead. The gospel isn't about our effort, even an effort so small as lifting one's head. I still wrestle with the divine mystery represented in that moment. We have not been saved by our own effort, but isn't faith effort? Isn't inviting Jesus into our lives effort? I don't know the answers to these questions, but I feel the answer when I see this dance in my head. Yes, she lifted her head at the invitation, but when Jesus came to her, she was beyond unable. It didn't matter, though. He crossed this gap too.

The chains exploded. The demons were blown out of sight. The whole world went white. Jesus and the girl embraced.

In parallel to the way her smallest effort revealed how overwhelmingly bound she was, Jesus' smallest effort, a gentle kiss on the forehead, immediately and completely set her free. It usually feels overindulgent and poorly paced to include every little detail of each thing I see, so some cuts are necessary, but I always regret not explaining how beautiful it looked as the chains broke.

Each link burst, splitting across the narrow part, one after the other. Each burst shot out a spatter of pure white sparks; each link disintegrated into particles of white light. They didn't even hit the ground. They vaporized into nothingness, utterly gone.

Maybe this is a picture of how complete the act of salvation is. Maybe God just likes making ugly things beautiful.

The demons were gone before the chains even fully disintegrated; they were a nonissue.

I don't know why the whole world disappeared around me. I don't know why I couldn't even see my own body. Maybe it was a picture of how that moment belonged solely to the two of them. Maybe this is why, when they hugged, I felt like such an intruder.

A massive hand came from above and touched me on the forehead.

I have no idea what this was about. Was it God anointing me to see people the way He does? That makes some sense with what happened afterward. Was He poking me out of the vision, like pushing a cat off furniture? I don't know. It was a big hand, though.

I started seeing every part of everyone's life if I looked at them for more than a second. I saw their potential and how far they were going to make it along that line of potential. I fell completely and totally in love with each one of them.

I saw it all. Not like a movie in fast-forward or a rapid-fire slideshow. It all came like memories I didn't have a moment before. It was like seeing a sibling or dear friend on their wedding day. You see them there in the moment, but you also see all the moments that led to the one in front of you. It wasn't exactly like that, but it was similar. I saw a lot of hard things that night. I saw a lot of beautiful things too. We all have storied lives, even when we are still young.

The "potential" thing always freaks people out a bit. You mean God has a plan for my life and I could mess it up? How much have I messed it up already? Am I messing it up right now?

Like the chains, this is a detail of the story that I often regret passing by. I saw this for each person like a tree. Each tree had thousands of branches, and each branch had leaves with pictures of each choice. I saw a pure white line run up each tree, following a singular path from the root to the tip of one branch. I knew this was the perfect plan of God. I then saw a stream of color flow up the trunk of the tree, filling in the branches. Sometimes it filled things along the path God's plan had laid, sometimes it did not.

Is this how God's plan works? What if I'm already way down the completely wrong branch? Am I too late already? Whoa, slow down, hypothetical reader. I'd be hesitant to draw too much of a conclusion about how God's plans work from this part of the vision. Why? Are you saying this part of the vision wasn't true? No, I don't think it's untrue, but I do think it's only a part of the truth.

This wasn't a vision about how God's plan works. It was a vision about God's love for the one, how great His love is for each individual person. I saw each person's entire life—the good, the bad, and all the spaces in between. I saw God's perfect plan for their life and how much they would fail to live up to it. Then I felt a love more intense than anything I had ever experienced flow through my entire being. This left no room for concern about their mistakes, past or future. This is not to say that these things did not matter or did not have consequences, only that His love was so massive that they were all as a pebble is to the whole of the earth.

———

I hope that this little exercise has been helpful, both to check in on how you are developing in your ability to understand the language of heaven and to mine a bit more out of this story. But I also wanted to take this opportunity to point out one more important facet of understanding the language of heaven, a rule of translation, if you will.

Whether you are reading the Bible, interpreting a dream, or trying to understand a vision, always be looking for the main message. This vision was vast and complex. There is a ton of room for overanalyzing and jumping to hundreds of conclusions based on every little detail. But it is hard to do this when we focus on the main message.

This vision was about God's love for the one. The vision with the woman in the alleyway and the angel fighting for her was about how painful and mysterious life is, and how despite this, God is good and heaven is fighting for us. The vision with the angel and the scroll that represented God's plans was about how vast and incredible God's intellect is, and how He can handle us just fine.

Are these perfect articulations of the main message of each of these visions? Probably not. But they are more refined than they were a year ago, or two, or ten. Looking for the main message is not about getting it perfect. It's about seeing the larger picture, the broader context. It can help keep us from treating molehills as mountains or being unable to see the forest through all those trees.

REFINING THE LANGUAGE

When I was a kid, I met one of my friends' older brothers during one of his visits from his time away at college. I had no idea how to talk to a college student, but I had seen a movie where someone asked one what they were studying, so that's what I asked.

"I'm studying English," he answered.

I furrowed my brow. "You haven't figured it out yet?"

He laughed at me. At the time I didn't know why, but now I understand. There's no ceiling on learning a language. You can learn enough to order dinner, make a joke, or have a fluent conversation, but even this is just the beginning. Every language is full of endless subtleties, nuances of use that go on and on and on. People spend their whole lives learning to master language through writing, speaking, poetry, song, and more.

There is no end to mastering the language of heaven. It is a framework of thinking that is built upon the nature of God, learning to think like our Father. We'll be working on this for the rest of our lives and, I think, into the rest of eternity.

We may never arrive, but I believe we can make massive strides.

But why should we do this? Is it for our own benefit? Is it to please God? These may be good reasons, but they aren't my main motivation.

A few weeks after I got back from the youth trip to Europe, one of the kids on the trip organized a get-together for everyone who had gone. She wanted us to worship together and pray. I went but stayed quiet for most of the evening. I was still reeling from what I had seen that last night in England. I hadn't told anyone about it yet, and I still wasn't sure what it meant for the struggle I was having with my faith.

One person played guitar with the handful of chords she knew, another sang mostly in key, and each kid took a turn speaking a passionate but clumsy prayer.

Then it happened again. I was looking at the girl playing guitar, and in a rush her entire life flashed before me. I saw the good. I saw the bad. I saw God's plan for her life. I saw what parts of it she'd choose and which parts she wouldn't. Again, the incomprehensible love flowed into me. Again, it began filling every corner of my psyche to the point of bursting. Again, I would do anything to express this love. And again, anything wasn't nearly enough.

My eyes darted from person to person. I was drawn to each of them, but looking at any of them was beautiful torture. Part of me realized, even though most of me was panicking, that it wasn't quite as overwhelming as last time. It was still more than I could possibly contain or express, but it came just a bit slower. In England it felt like every time I looked at someone, my soul was sucked off the edge of Niagara Falls and left churning at the bottom. This time it was only a trip down category-five rapids.

A voice at the back of my mind spoke, one that sounded very much like the one that had said, "He sees no one but her."

This time it said, "Just speak."

So I did. I prophesied over each person in the room. It was the only thing that I knew how to do that might get anywhere close to expressing the love that I was feeling.

It didn't, but it was good. I had never prophesied over that many people at once, only nineteen, but it was a lot to me back then. Each person seemed blessed, but I left feeling more than a little empty. It was like trying to do a crayon drawing of a sunset or playing one of Beethoven's symphonies on a kazoo; something made it across, but it was painful to see how much didn't.

Three months later it happened again. We were at a prayer meeting, and I started seeing people's lives and feeling the same overwhelming love. I prophesied again, and it was good again, but there was still so much missing.

It happened again with a stranger while I was at the store. I wasn't sure if it confused her or made her day, but I did my best.

It kept happening, not more frequently, but consistently. I picked up my old prophetic books again. I had to learn how to express this love better. I started reading the Bible again. If I was going to express this love, then I needed to understand where it came from. I started practicing the prophetic with others again. I had to grow because this love was worth growing for. I turned my hobby of writing into a dedicated practice; I had to learn how to communicate this love.

I started studying the language of heaven.

Should you learn the language of heaven for your own benefit? Yes, it will benefit your life in ways that you cannot possibly imagine. Should you learn the language of heaven to please God? Well, I would modify this just a bit by saying that you should learn the language of heaven so that you have intimate and personal knowledge of just how pleased He is with you.

These are both wonderful reasons to learn the language of heaven. But I have spent my life learning the language of heaven so that I can be a part of showing people what heaven looks like. I want to be able to show people who God is to the absolute best of my ability. I want to learn how to represent Him in every aspect of life. I want to learn how to treat my whole life as sacred, to live fully in the world, but live fully by the Spirit.

If we do this—grow daily in our knowledge of the culture and nature of God—then we won't just be learning a language. We'll be bringing heaven to earth.

CONCLUSION

I N THIS BOOK we have explored how the spirit realm works, we have been learning how to understand the language of heaven, and we have been discovering how we fit in all this as spiritual beings. Before we depart one another's company, I wanted to take one last opportunity to take a step back and take a broader view.

What is secular? Traditionally this word has been used to denote the difference between traditional work and ministerial work. I'm sure we all draw these lines differently in our heads, some consciously and some unconsciously. Is your time at church on Sunday sacred and everything else secular? If you sell cars, is that a secular job? What if you work for a nonprofit that feeds the homeless? Is that secular if it is run by a nonreligious organization and sacred if it is run by a church?

I hope that in our time together you have come to realize that everything we do is spiritual. If everything we do is spiritual, then does that mean everything we do is sacred? That can't be true because some of what we do is harmful to ourselves and others. So, then, is the line a measure of morals? If not, then what is it?

I would like to do something that I normally avoid and try to provide a definition for these three words, not because I think these are the right definitions, but because I think they are helpful.

I would like to suggest that anything we do for the glory of God is sacred and anything that we do not is secular.

Secular doesn't necessarily mean evil, just not unto the glory of God. This is a helpful framework because it broadens the horizons of how glory can be expressed. God's glory can be revealed through art, literature, industry, education, invention, relationship, family, religion, politics, government, nature, technology, civilization, and all other means yet to be discovered. But His glory is not always revealed in these things.

I believe this is a helpful framework for broadly understanding how the spirit realm interacts with all these aspects of creation and how each of them can be secular or sacred. But how do we fit into all this? What does it mean to be a spirit?

A Dream and a Garden

One Saturday afternoon, I was out in front of my house, watching my kids ride their bikes in circles in the driveway. I was just thinking about going inside to get a drink of water when I turned and saw Jesus at the end of my driveway. As you already know, this was not the first time I had seen Jesus, but it was the first time I saw Him like this.

He was more than twenty feet tall, clothed in robes of layered purple and gold, adorned with layers of precious metals and gems. His head and face were so bright that it made the sun look dim. My knees shook, and I felt incredibly small. The authority that resonated from Him was overwhelming, but I could also feel kindness woven between the emanating waves of power. I felt a deeper understanding of what it meant for Him to be both the Lion and the Lamb.

My children didn't seem to be aware that the King of kings was standing next to our mailbox. They continued riding their bikes up and down the driveway, turning just in front of His massive feet. I thought I saw a smile as they rode past, but His face was too bright to be certain.

It was then that I noticed there was something behind Him, something tall and rectangular. Tall black rows of drawers, so tall that they blocked out the sun, sat in perfectly spaced rows that ran all the way up and down the street in front of my house. Each had dozens of large square drawers, about the same size of those found in a file cabinet. It looked like the road in front of my house had suddenly been turned into the records department in an old office building or library.

"What is this?" I asked out loud.

"It is a graveyard." His voice shook my bones and held them together at the same time.

A graveyard? What does that mean? I thought. *Like with dead people? That's weird. This is weird. What is going on here?*

I assumed that Jesus could hear my thoughts, but I didn't expect Him to answer. I have been living with these kinds of experiences long enough to get a feel for what is expected. This is what caused me to instinctually ask out loud, "What is this?"

I don't know why, exactly, but some encounters have a prescribed flow and cadence. It doesn't mean that you have to say everything perfectly or that you're going to get smote for asking the wrong question. But again, like the flow of a dance, there are steps to be followed.

So I felt for the rhythm and asked the next question.

"Why is it here?"

"It is a graveyard of dreams."

I looked down the road in both directions. The rows of tall drawers went as far as I could see both ways, each higher than the nearby trees. Confused at why thousands of dead dreams would be in a small suburban neighborhood on the south side of Atlanta, I asked again, "Why is it here?"

"This graveyard covers the entire earth. There is nowhere that it is not."

I looked back and saw rows of identical drawers across my backyard, into the forest behind my house, and beyond. I turned back to look at Jesus and suddenly saw rows of drawers on either side of me, as well as either side of Him. We were in the endless maze of tall drawers.

Why would people's dreams be piled up in drawers? Why would there be so many? I waited and felt for the rhythm again. Then a thought occurred to me.

"Whose dreams are these?"

I felt Jesus smile, though I still could not see His face clearly. "They are Mine."

As He spoke, a series of images flashed through my mind. I saw flashes of other towns, cities, and nations. I saw the rows of shelves and drawers covering every part of every one of them. There was no place on the earth that God did not have a dream for. The thought didn't feel new, necessarily, but the depth and clarity behind it did. Every city, every home, every part of every society in every country across every part of the world—He had dreams for them all.

With this knowledge still settling in my mind, I looked more closely at the drawers. The understanding brought the vision into clearer focus. I quickly noticed that there were two kinds of drawers. Some of the drawers were plain, flat gray with a steel handle. The others were beautifully adorned, made of marble and gilded with brass and gold. Some of these even had flowers or ribbons tucked into the handles. Something about the gray ones felt sad, hollow, and lifeless. Something about the gilded ones felt joyful, peaceful, and complete.

I turned to Jesus, and He answered my question before it left my lips. "Not all of My dreams come true."

He reached down to one of the low shelves and pulled one of the gilded drawers open just a few inches. I approached the open drawer and was shocked to see feet inside. I tilted my head to look a little deeper into the drawer. There was a person, a whole person, lying on their back.

"All of My dreams are fulfilled through My children," He said.

Again, I have been doing this long enough that I knew this was not literally a person or a ghost or anything like that, but this vision represented something that was very literal: the dreams of God and the people who had dedicated their lives to fulfilling those dreams.

He opened one of the plain gray drawers. It was full of papers, hundreds of them, filling the drawer from front to back. He flipped through some of the pages. The best way I can describe the papers in the drawer is to compare them to a business plan. He had a plan, a dream, and He had accounted for every single detail. He had counted every cost, readied for every contingency, and mapped out every part of every step. It was a perfect and complete plan, but it had not come to pass.

I looked up at the thousands of drawers above and beside me and realized that there were more dull gray drawers than there were gilded ones—a lot more. A spike of fury and sorrow shot through me. It was sudden and overwhelming. I could see all the good, all the glory that God wanted to accomplish throughout history where none of His sons or daughters stepped up to release His purposes. I could see all the hurting and broken for whom He had laid out plans for healing and redemption, but no child of God answered the call. He had plans for every place on the earth and every moment of history, but so many had passed by.

Without thinking, I whipped my head around, looked at Jesus, and shouted, "Then why do You dream at all?"

He paused for a moment, and the ferocity in my heart steadied. He responded firmly, confidently, and kindly, "I never stop believing in My children, no matter how often My hope is deferred."

I stood for a minute, letting myself calm the rest of the way. Then Jesus said, "Would you like to see yours?"

I looked up and said, "Sure."

All at once He reached up and grabbed the middle of the shelves and pulled, moving the whole rack as if it were on a slider. The wall of drawers flew by until He slapped down His palm and stopped it.

This new section of drawers was different. Every one of them was gilded, and all of them were open. Immediately I knew that these were the dreams that were neither fulfilled nor unfulfilled, the dreams that were waiting for His children to arrive.

A drawer sat just in front of my chest. I knew it was mine even before He reached out to pull it all the way open. The inside had the padding and cloth of a fancy coffin. I was suddenly struck by how narrow the drawer was.

"It seems a bit small," I said, looking down at myself and wondering if I would fit.

"That's right. It is small," Jesus said, resting a hand on my shoulder. "There's no room for your dreams in there, only Mine."

I turned to look at Him.

"It's all right," He said. "I'll hold your dreams for you."

It was neither a promise that He would add my dreams to the drawer nor a promise that He would not. It was an invitation to trust Him.

Before I could hesitate or think, I stepped into the drawer.

The moment my shoe touched the bottom of the drawer, I was completely blinded by an open vision. I could feel the ground underneath my feet and hear the sound of my children's bicycle tires on the pavement, but I could not see either. Though I felt a spike of parental concern, I remembered how, years ago, I'd had a similar experience with an open vision while driving my car. God had kept me safe then; it would have been silly not to trust Him now.

In the open vision I found myself suspended thousands of feet in the air. I looked down and saw a city far below me, less distant than if I were in an airplane, but only just. I looked to my right and saw hundreds of people suspended in midair just like I was. I looked to the left and saw the same: hundreds of people hanging in the air in a line, facing the same direction.

I looked back and saw Jesus, just as magnificent and glorious as before, floating in the air behind us all. As soon as I looked, the light that surrounded His head spread down, illuminating every part of His body. He grew brighter and brighter, so bright that I could no longer look at Him directly. As I turned away, I saw that beams of light were emanating from Him, thick beams of pure white luminescence. I followed the trails of light and realized that there was a beam of light pointed at each person that hung in the air. Then I saw what was happening when the light struck each person.

At first the light split like it would through a prism, bending and revealing all the colors hidden in the white, but it did not stop there. Each of the colors split, bending into more colors, and more after that. They bent further, making oscillating geometric designs of every shape, size, and color, spinning great masterworks of mathematics and architecture. They split more, bending into the organic patterns of leaves, snowflakes, tree roots, and flickering flames, creating massive waterfalls of living and moving art. Again and again it split into unending forms of color and light more beautiful than I had ever seen. The light bent differently through each person, making each cascading fractal of color utterly unique.

Then I heard Jesus speak again, His voice closer than if He were whispering in my ear. "Look ahead. See what it does." His voice glowed with the pride of a master craftsman revealing a completed work.

I looked ahead, and my whole body went numb.

The rivers of transforming light were soaring out to every corner of the world, changing every place that they touched. I saw businesses being started, succeeding, and expanding, every member of the company, from the greatest to the least, glowing with wholeness and satisfaction. I saw books being written, then turned into films, then being seen across every corner of the world. Some represented Jesus explicitly and led people directly to Him; some represented Jesus implicitly and prepared the hearts of millions to recognize Him when they saw Him. I saw churches where signs, wonders, and miracles were the norm. They trained and equipped healthy sons and daughters to train and equip more healthy sons and daughters.

I saw every facet of society and every son or daughter of God who was sent to release His dream for glory in that place.

I turned and looked to another part of the world, and I saw pain. I saw sorrow. I heard every voice crying out. I heard every curse thrown out by those who had been left broken and abandoned. Then I felt the impossible blend of wrath and compassion well up from Jesus—compassion at the pain, wrath at the suffering. Then I saw men and women leading armies of people to feed the hungry, serve the broken, and heal the wounded. I saw mothers and fathers running to rescue abandoned children. I saw friends seeking the lonely. I saw hands reaching out to the rejected.

I saw every hurt, every pain, and every sorrow that had ever occurred on the earth and the son or daughter of God who was sent to be His answer.

I saw the plans and plots of the enemy, the culmination of his plans for culture, society, and the people within them. Every one of them dried to a husk and crumbled to ash, powerless in the face of God's unending light.

I watched for hours. The light never stopped. I watched for days. The light never stopped. It only grew as more took their places as beacons of God's glory.

Time went by. I blinked, and then Jesus was standing in front of me.

"Is this what is going to happen? Is this what could happen? Your light released through Your people, transforming the world?"

He smiled. "It is already happening."

I thought back to all the gray drawers, thousands of dreams throughout history, so many incomplete or ignored. The feeling of anger began to rise again, frustration at those who would leave God's dreams unfulfilled.

"Stop," Jesus said. My anger vanished in an instant. He stepped forward and rested a hand on my shoulder again. "You decide whether you want to step in. That is all. That is enough."

I blinked again, and He was gone. I stood in my driveway, my children riding their bikes in a circle. I looked at the time. Less than two minutes had passed.

What does it mean to be a spirit? What are we supposed to do in the spirit realm? There's probably more than one answer, but this is my favorite answer to both questions: to be a bearer of the image of God.

In the beginning God created. All that He created was good. He created mankind in His image, in His likeness. He placed them in a garden. He called them to rule over all the creatures of creation, to subdue the earth and multiply.

This is our sacred duty. What does it mean to subdue the earth? Again, I think there are a lot of good answers to this question, and several bad ones as well. But the answer I like is to shape the earth to magnify God's glory.

What on earth magnifies God's glory? Anything we do unto His glory.

This is clearly an oversimplified answer. But like a compass, while it can't tell us exactly how to get where we are going, it can help orient us along the way. Doing things unto God's glory is not as simple as thanking Him at the end of a football game or praying before you go to work. It is as complex and all-consuming as learning the language of heaven. But it is worth discovering how you are designed to bring God's glory into the earth. I have seen how beautiful it is when people do.

NOTES

EPIGRAPH

1. *Merriam-Webster*, s.v. "secular," accessed November 2, 2022, https://www.merriam-webster.com/dictionary/secular; *Merriam-Webster*, s.v. "sacred," accessed November 2, 2022, https://www.merriam-webster.com/dictionary/sacred; *Merriam-Webster*, s.v. "spirit," accessed November 2, 2022, https://www.merriam-webster.com/dictionary/spirit.

CHAPTER 7

1. C. S. Lewis, *The Weight of Glory: And Other Addresses* (New York: HarperOne, 1980), 33.
2. Lewis, *The Weight of Glory*, 33.